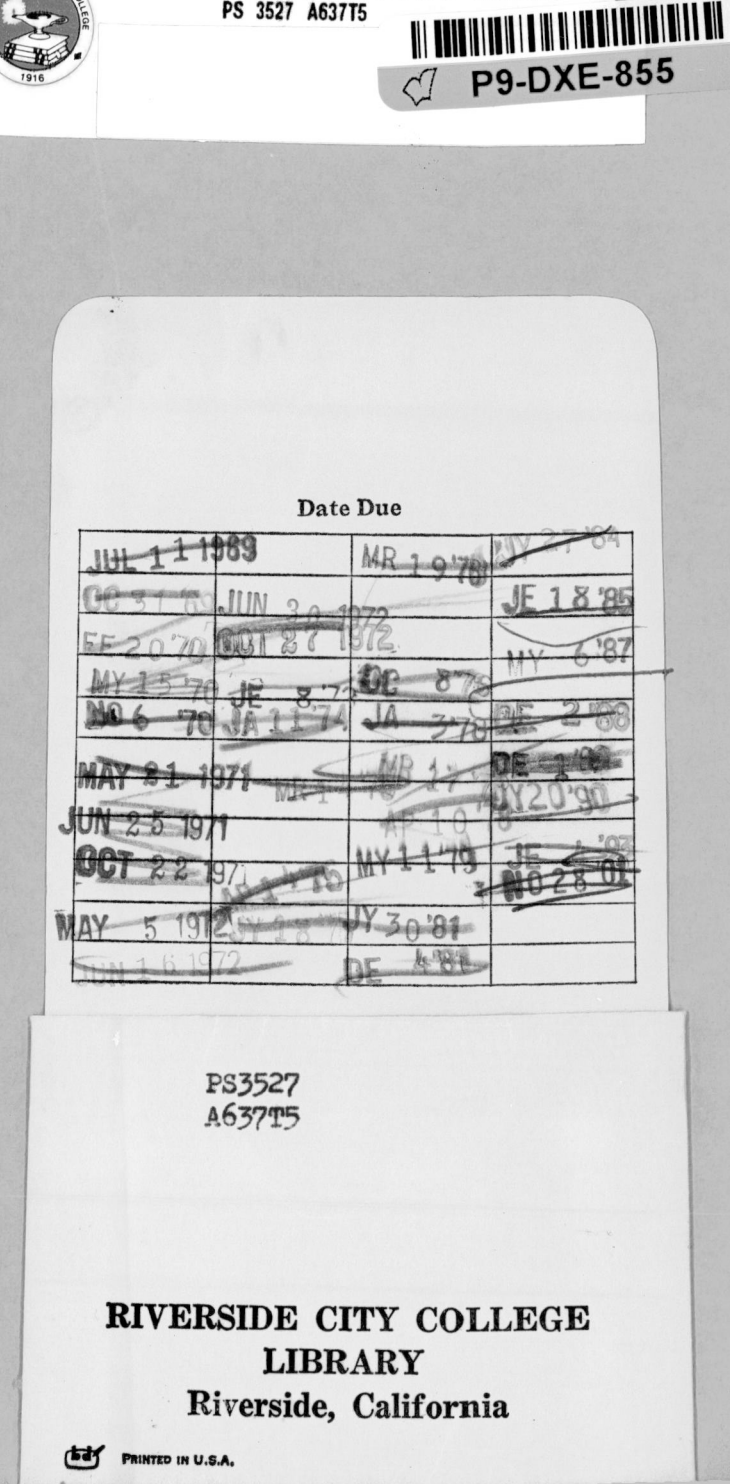

Date Due

JUL 11 1969	MR 19 '70	MY 27 '84
OC 31 '69	JUN 30 1972	JE 18 '85
FE 20 '70	OCT 27 1972	MY 6 '87
MY 15 '70	JE 8 '7	DE 8 '7	MY 6 '87
NO 6 70	JA 11 74	JA 27 78	DE 2 88
MAY 21 1971	MR 1	MR 17	DE 1 89
JUN 25 1971		AP 10 7	JY 20 '90
OCT 22 1971		MY 11 79	JE '93
			NO 28 01
MAY 5 1972		JY 30 '81	
JUN 16 1972		DE 4 '81	

BOOKS BY OGDEN NASH

I'M A STRANGER HERE MYSELF

GOOD INTENTIONS

MANY LONG YEARS AGO

VERSUS

FAMILY REUNION

THE PRIVATE DINING ROOM AND OTHER NEW VERSES

YOU CAN'T GET THERE FROM HERE

VERSES FROM 1929 ON (SELECTIONS FROM PUBLISHED WORKS)

EVERYONE BUT THEE AND ME

MARRIAGE LINES:
Notes of a Student Husband

SANTA GO HOME:
A Case History for Parents

THERE'S ALWAYS ANOTHER WINDMILL

THERE'S ALWAYS
ANOTHER WINDMILL

THERE'S ALWAYS
ANOTHER WINDMILL

BY

OGDEN NASH

WITH DECORATIONS BY
JOHN ALCORN

LITTLE, BROWN AND COMPANY • BOSTON • TORONTO

LIBRARY OF CONGRESS CATALOG CARD NO. 68-25903

FIRST EDITION

Many of these poems first appeared in magazines and are
reprinted through the courtesy of the following: *The
Atlantic, Good Housekeeping, Gourmet, Harper's, Holiday,
House Beautiful, Ladies Home Journal, Look, McCall's,
New Republic, New York Herald Tribune Book Review, The
New Yorker, Playboy, Punch, The Reporter, Saturday Eve-
ning Post, Saturday Review, Sports Illustrated, Status, Ven-
ture,* and *Vogue.*

*Published simultaneously in Canada
by Little, Brown & Company (Canada) Limited*

PRINTED IN THE UNITED STATES OF AMERICA

Once more for Frances.
Who else is there?

CONTENTS

SONGS OF INNOCENCE

HOW PLEASANT TO APE MR. LEAR

SONGS OF EXPERIENCE

[xii]

SONGS OF INNOCENCE

ALL GOOD AMERICANS
GO TO LAROUSSE
OR, I DON'T PRETEND TO BE MOLIÈRE
THAN THOU

I reckon it is nearly fifty years to the day
Since I first repeated after Mademoiselle the deceptively
    simple preliminaries *"je suis," "tu es," "il est."*
Half a century later, almost to the dot,
That is still about as far into the French language as I have
    got.
Of my own shortcomings I will not be a whitewasher or
    launderer;
After thorough exposure to teachers, tutors, and tourism, I
    remain a monolingual maunderer.
At convivial gatherings where such gay songs as "Alouette"
    and "Auprès de Ma Blonde" are sung —
Well, I can but mumble that *le chat* has got my tongue,
A phrase I pronounce with confidence and aplomb
Only because that particular *chat* is a tom.
Indeed, where I really bust a *bretelle,* or suspender,
Is when I wrestle with the French indiscriminate parceling
    out of gender.
This confusion once led me into the ultimate *faux pas:*
I found myself exclaiming *"Oh, le le!"* instead of *"Oh, là là!"*
Small wonder that from French I have learned to keep my
    distance;
It has mocked itself of me too often in the years between the
    early P.S. 59 and this late *pièce de* resistance.

What if I thus bar myself from glittering *salons,* where the
    talk is all of Racine and Sacha Guitry and Réjane?
Right at home *il y a* Tennessee Williams and *il y a* Marlon
    Brando and Elia Kazan.
Also, I take consolation in the likelihood that at this very
    moment fifty million Frenchmen may be in parallel
    bewildering plights
As they try to differentiate between Fenimore Cooper's
    Peaux-Rouges and Erskine Caldwell's po' whites.

JOHN PEEL, SHAKE HANDS WITH 37 MAMAS

Bishop DeWolfe Greets 37 Debutantes on L. I.

. . . At the cathedral, the debutantes . . . were escorted up
the aisle . . . to where the Right Rev. James P. DeWolfe was
enthroned on the bishop's chair before the altar. Each girl
received a medallion and a blessing from Bishop DeWolfe.
            — The Times.

Oh, blithe it is to bless the hounds
Before the hunt begins,
That they may blood the wicked fox
Unshriven of his sins.

What will avail his wily ways,
His heathenish heroics,
Against such Anglican battle hymns
As "Tallyho!" and "Yoicks!"?

No more his magic bag of tricks
Shall serve the crafty stunter;

[4]

His mask and brush this day shall prove
That God is with the hunter.

So let us start a sterner chase
Before momentum ebbs;
If bishops bless a pack of hounds,
Why not a pack of debs?

Thus Heav'n's good will is now invoked
For maiden, not for bachelor;
Small wonder that he feels depressed
As tongue beneath the spatula.

Small wonder that his blood runs chill
As maids receive the benison,
For he, today a running stag,
Tomorrow may be venison.

At each soprano "View halloo!"
His palms grow cold and damp;
In vain he doubles on his tracks
To club or fishing camp.

The pack is snapping at his heels
In virginal battalions;
No ruse or stratagem can prevail
'Gainst blessings and medallions.

Behold Diana's trophy room,
Aswarm with little nippers.
Beneath the fox's brush and mask
We find a pipe and slippers.

THE DAY OF THE LOCUST
OR, WHOSE WEDDING IS THIS ANYWAY?

At 4 o'clock the sky is cloudless, it looks as if the storm
    would abstain.
At 4:05 the organ strikes up "Here Comes the Bride," and
    at 4:06 here comes the rain.
No chance of the guests spreading over the country club
    lawn, their gala dress unwrinkled and immaculate,
Now perforce they must all under the marquee coagulate.
The limousines splash up to the club, the members of the
    wedding disembark,
The dripping churchgoers creep into the receiving line two
    by two, like animals entering the ark.
They find the queue headed by the locusts who skipped the
    ceremony, who have been here since 3:30, their tongues
    hanging down to their laps,
But they think they can get away with it, perhaps,
And any suspicion of their truancy they attempt to cancel
By exclaiming over the beauty of the flowers in the chancel.
An obvious lie;
Their feet are dry.
It is these locusts who swarm to the buffet, where they es-
    tablish a monopoly,
They hold it against the starving but still polite church-
    goers as the Spartans held the pass at Thermopylae.
Their eyes are wild as those of hippies high on pot, or joy
    grass;
With bare fingers they tear every truffle from the foie gras;
Napoleons and kossuths

Vanish like so many Tootsie Rolls and Baby Ruths.
For the preceding week they have been drooling, dieting,
and reducing;
Now they are here not for any love of the happy couple, but,
as Mr. Wodehouse would say, purely for the browsing
and sluicing.
They gulp champagne by the jeroboam,
And they are the last to go hoam.
My admiration and gratitude would on Amy Vanderbilt be
focused
If she could devise a way to retain the wedding and elimi-
nate the locust.

IF THERE WERE NO ENGLAND, COUNTRY LIFE COULD INVENT IT

I, lover of names, admirer of houses,
Eagerly scanning the pages of *Country Life,*
Crown-jewel box of both,
Suddenly hit the jackpot, gave a barbaric yawp.
For I saw, I saw "In South Bucks, placed on the edge of
    Common,
Charming family home, dating from 17th Century,"
Mine, mine for the asking, or equivalent dollars or sterling!
Offered, proffered discreetly
By "Hetherington & Secrett,
In conjunction with Swannell & Sly."
A hall has it, and "cloakrooms, and reception rooms 3 or 4,
Kitchen, 6 bedrooms (no attics),"
And, best of all, "2 bathrooms
(Including separately entered suite for relatives)."
This "freehold for sale by auction
(Also by private treaty)"
Through Hetherington & Secrett and their friends Swannell
    & Sly.
I would not wound Mr. Hetherington
Nor bypass Mr. Swannell,
But had I the tanners and florins, the guineas, the ponies,
    the monkeys,
I'd draw up *two* private treaties —
The one with Mr. Secrett,
The other with Mr. Sly.
If I could not meet their terms
(Which mention a "Low Reserve"),
I might make a modest bid for at least those six no attics.
I would go considerably higher, of course,
For the "separately entered suite for relatives."

[9]

GOD BLESS THE GIDEONS
OR,
THERE'S ALWAYS THE KING JAMES VERSION

High near the mountain or low near the ocean,
Hard by the spa, it's the same old hotel,
Born of a Middle Victorian notion,
Reaching full stature, with ell tacked on ell.

Septuagenarians crowd its verandas,
Leathery lady and fragile old man,
Sunning like lizards or dozing like pandas,
Dreaming of dinner, American plan.

Far past the TV room, far past the cardroom,
Deep in a cranny encompassed by nooks,
Dim as a dungeon and grim as a guardroom,
There is the library, these are the books —

Gone the gay jackets with blurbs parading,
Along the spine the titles are fading:
If Winter Comes, by A. S. M. Hutch.,
Castle Craneycrow, George Barr McCutch.,
The Amateur Gentleman, Jeffery Farnol,
Hilda Lessways, Bennett, Arnol',
Calvin Coolidge, C. Bascom Slemp,
Over the Top, Arthur Guy Emp.,
The Green Hat, Michael Arlen,
Blind Raftery, Donn Byrne's Irish darlin'.
Here lie Cosmo Hamilton, A. Hamilton Gibbs,
Joan Lowell, Trader Horn and their fabulous fibs,

The Art of Thinking, a tattered *Freckles,*
And an early, early Beverley Nichols.

Forty years on, when, afar and asunder,
Ashes are those who are reading today,
Strangers will gaze on our leavings with wonder,
Sum up an era and turn to croquet.

Behind glass doors not wholly hidden,
A literary kitchen midden,
The musty rubble of a race
Which fed on Kinsey and *Peyton Place.*
De Sade and *Valley of the Dolls* consort
With *Story of O* and *The Chapman Report,*
The *Tropics,* and other tins of sex;
Also, *The Agony and the Ecs.,*
Advise and Consent, by a Mr. Drury,
That life of Harlow, unhappy houri,
And, yes, *How Probate to Avoid,*
And *Papa Hemingway,* not by Freud;
Memoirs of Getty, mystery Croesus,
And *Are You Running with Me, Jesus?*
In a corner, *This Is My Beloved,*
Penned by a twentieth-century Ovid,
And at one end, cleared by the courts,
A mildewed batch of Grove Press orts.

Golden pens and royalties must,
As chimney sweepers, come to dust.

A VISITOR FROM PORLOCK,
BUT, ALAS, NO XANADU

I am not an organist but I am weary and ill at ease and also
    in the doldrums;
My mind is cluttered with folderoldrums.
I have lived through a visit from a lady who is best described
    as overflowing;
She is full of truisms but she is not like a truism, because a
    truism goes without saying, but she says without going.
She had a bee in her bonnet and the bit in her teeth and a
    flow of banalities impervious to repulse,
And my attention strayed, with psychedelic results.
I wondered if anyone wishing to hear what the morrow's
    weather will be knows or cares about the meaning of
    degree days and dew points,
And I thought of the songwriter who assumed the role of
    the Creator with an insane cry of "Let there be you —
    and let there be me! Let there be oysters under the
    sea!" but who failed to specify whether Cape Cods or
    Blue Points.
Indeed, my vagrant thoughts were many,
And one of them lingered on the distinguished poet who re-
    cently wrote that he would "dream of small white stars
    falling forever in darkness like dandruff," and I asked
    myself if this phrase could be a subconscious tribute to
    the late *Daily Mirror*'s immortal bard, Nick Kenny.
Nick Kenny could come up with a simile in the face of over-
    whelming odds,
And in his simile it was not stars falling, but snowflakes, and
    they were like not just anyone's dandruff, but God's.
It occurred to me that I find unidentified flying objects less
    menacing than flying objects all too easily identified by
    the kind of screaming shock that may one day accom-

pany the transformation of Croton-on-Hudson into
Hudson-on-Croton;
The UFO's at least are silent and never have plagued me
into comments that would be, should I quote them
verbatim, verboten.
I deplored the fact that there is so little fresh orange juice
in a world overstocked with electric squeezers,
And I wished someone would devise a better way to dispose
of the surplus cotton crop than cramming it into aspirin
bottles from which it must be extracted with pins and
nail files and tweezers.
Even from contemplating the unfair state alcoholic-beverage
laws that discriminate against youth I did not shrink,
And I concluded that anybody old enough to picket the
White House is old enough to drink.
It was at this point in my centripetal escapism that the lady
arose, and I gathered that her theme had been akin to
a coroner's —
She had been pronouncing the country dead owing to an
overdose of foreigners.
She told me that there was no wool over her eyes and that
she was nobody's fool,
And she knew for a fact that there were forty Greek students
in that bastion of blue-blooded, red-blooded American
boyhood, St. Paul's School.
She then dropped the final bomb that completed her mis-
sion;
She informed me that the daughter of a mutual friend was
frequenting discothèques with a naturalized citizen
who had been a bootlicker during Prohibition.
I escorted her to the door with Old World courtesy and a
Gallic *"Au'voir,"*
And told myself to cheer up, it might have been Simone de
Beauvoir.

[13]

THE CRICKET

I love to hear a cricket in my house.
Not so my spouse.
To me he caps the comfort of the hearth
When leaves, once scarlet,
Spread like a wet brown carpet
Across the first thin crackle of the frosty earth.

She owns his chirp is homely, but takes him for
A predator,
Devourer of her precious rugs and spreads.
Old wives' tale has it
He'll sack her neat-piled closet,
Leaving her only lavender, and linen shreds.

I know the cricket
Is not so wicked,
And even if he were,
And I his grim Javert,
He'd escape my foot, although my hearing sharp is,
For be he friend
Or ravenous fiend,
You prod and poke and peek
In futile hide and seek;
Your cricket is sly, he's never where his chirp is.

No, you'll never come on cricket and chirp together,
Evasive tactics bewilder his pursuer.
So much for war, but when it comes to love,
How does his wooed one ever find her wooer?

JUST HOLMES AND ME,
AND MNEMOSYNE, MAKES THREE

I am told that my character has as many layers as an onyx,
But one layer is missing, which is an aptitude for mnemonics.
Mnemosyne (daughter of Uranus and Gaea, date of birth
destroyed in fire at Alexandria) was the goddess of
memory,
So she never said "Hail, Amory!" to a minor deity whose
name was Emory.
She became a mother by Zeus — as what nubile Grecian
female didn't? — and the children turned out to be the
Muses, who later on helped Homer with their reminis-
cences of Achilles and Hector,
And she needed her innate talent, because she had nine
names to remember when she summoned them to their
ambrosia and nectar.
Me, I can never be elected to any office, because I am near-
sighted and frequently forget the face of an acquaint-
ance, and, worse, I invariably forget the name,
So I am solaced by the discovery that my lifelong hero Mr.
Sherlock Holmes was once the same.
In "The Adventure of the Speckled Band" (*The Complete
Sherlock Holmes*, Doubleday, 1953), the proposed vic-
tim of a fiendish plot introduces herself on page 294 as
Miss Helen Stoner, stepdaughter of Dr. Grimesby Roy-
lott, of Stoke Moran,
An unpleasant man,
Yet on page 299 Holmes says to her, "Miss Roylott . . . you
are screening your stepfather," a slip that Miss Stoner
left uncorrected, either through tact or because her
mind was upon her approaching wedding,

For she had recently become betrothed to Mr. Percy Armitage, second son of Mr. Armitage, of Crane Water, near Reading.

Well, whatever caused Holmes's error and Miss Stoner's overlooking it, I have this reflection to cheer me as I step from the mounting block to the saddle of my high-wheeled bike:

Great minds forget alike.

IF HE WERE ALIVE TODAY, MAYHAP, MR. MORGAN WOULD SIT ON THE MIDGET'S LAP

"Beep-beep.

BANKERS TRUST AUTOMOBILE LOAN
You'll find a banker at Bankers Trust"
(Advertisement in N.Y. *Times*)

When comes my second childhood,
As to all men it must,
I want to be a banker
Like the banker at Bankers Trust.
I wouldn't ask to be president,
Or even assistant veep,
I'd only ask for a kiddie car
And permission to go beep-beep.

The banker at Chase Manhattan,
He bids a polite Good-day;
The banker at Immigrant Savings
Cries Scusi! and Olé!
But I'd be a sleek Ferrari
Or perhaps a joggly jeep,
And scooting around at Bankers Trust,
Beep-beep, I'd go, beep-beep.

The trolley car used to say clang-clang
And the choo-choo said toot-toot,
But the beep of the banker at Bankers Trust
Is every bit as cute.
Miaow, says the cuddly kitten,

Baa, says the woolly sheep,
Oink, says the piggy-wiggy,
And the banker says beep-beep.

So I want to play at Bankers Trust
Like a hippety-hoppy bunny,
And best of all, oh best of all,
With really truly money.
Now grown-ups dear, it's nightie-night
Until my dream comes true,
And I bid you a happy boop-a-doop
And a big beep-beep adieu.

HOW MANY MILES TO THE
DEAD LETTER OFFICE?

I
A MODEST PROPOSAL TO
ABOLISH THE SALIVA TEST

I have a helpful suggestion for our melancholy Postmaster
General,
The financial condition of whose department he informs us
is truly hellish and Gehennaral.
There is one thing I deem less pleasing than a jolly jolly
M.C. or toastmaster,
Namely, a melancholy postmaster,
Because a postmaster suffering from melancholium,
He is apt to shed tears all over the Director of the Budget's
linoleum.
Therefore, if he will but say Okay, the modern German
equivalent of *Ja wohl,*
I can show him how to turn the ink in his ledgers from red
to a black as black as the night from pole to pole.
At present he is under the misapprehension that a negative
approach will lead him out of the financial thicket,
He economizes by giving us a stamp backed by a bargain-
counter non-adhesive glue that falls off the envelope no
matter how many times you lick it.
I think he should accentuate the positive and thereby earn
an honest extra buck,
He could easily sell a roll of magic transparent tape with
every sheet of stamps, which when the stamp you stick
on the envelope unsticks will keep it stuck.
Another thing the magic transparent tape would do,
It would reunite those portions of Presidents' faces that have
been torn apart because the perforations don't go all
the way through.

[20]

I believe that these rolls of tape would bring in many golden
    eggs with no danger of killing the goose,
Because though we would pay through the nose for them
    that is a method of paying that has long been in com-
    mon use.

II
STAMP TOO BIG FOR LETTER,
MUST BE FOR ALBUM

If the Postmaster General, in order to transmute his bud-
    getary woes into budgetary bliss, is looking for a cata-
    lyst,
Well, there is a simple formula: Stop wasting my money by
    catering to the philatelist.
What does the philatelist gloat over as Con Edison gloats
    over its volts and watts and amps?
Issue after issue of commemorative stamps.
And what have the following in common: James and Marilyn
    Monroe, Rock and Henry Hudson, Jefferson and Bette
    Davis, Rutherford B. and Helen Hayes, and the Taylors,
    Elizabeth and Zachary?
Just that their likenesses are bound to turn up someday in
    this mishmash of costly and pretentious quackery.
Yes, someday our letters will carry their features as sculpted
    by the current Rodin or St. Gaudens,
Because someday everybody else's features will have been
    used except possibly Lizzie Borden's.
I shouldn't be surprised if the amount squandered on en-
    graving and printing these superfluous monstrosities
    would launch a satellite,
And who and nobody else wants them? The philatelite.
Please cease this practice, Mr. Postmaster General, in the
    interests of economy,
Just keep on issuing the same old stamps, and you and I will
    live together within our means and in perfect bonhomie.

THE ENTRAPMENT OF
JOHN ALDEN
OR, WE PAINT THE LILY,
WE BEARD MR. LONGFELLOW

Once there was a Pilgrim Father named Miles Standish,

Because despite many misconceptions few Pilgrim Fathers were named Praise-God Barebones or something equally outlandish.

Miles Standish was ordinarily a direct man, but in affairs of the heart he was inclined to crawfish,

Indeed, he might have been termed Standish-offish.

He had moved from Plymouth to Duxbury, and he had a friend who was a born bachelor named John Alden

Who had also moved to Duxbury, though he might have done better to plump for Nahant or Saugus or Malden.

Well, Miles Standish fell in love with a Pilgrim maiden named Priscilla Mullens,

But whenever he approached her she fell into a fit of the sulks or sullens,

And he was afraid that if he offered her marriage in person she would grow even acider,

So the upshot was that he persuaded John Alden to be his ambassador,

And the offshoot of the upshot was that Priscilla welcomed John Alden as Penelope might have welcomed Odysseus

And she baked him a pumpkin pie that was simply de-lysseus,

And she evinced a frightening tendency to mingle,

And when he transmitted Miles Standish's proposal to her she asked him why he didn't speak for himself, but he really had nothing to say for himself except that he enjoyed being single.

Had he been a Method actor preparing for a play set in Greenpoint he could have told himself, "I can ad lib dis,"
But now with the image of Miles Standish looking over one shoulder and an amorous maiden snuggling against the other he stood silent between Priscilla and Charybdis.
This silence resulted in a union which eventually produced eleven children, several of them born in August,
And a recently discovered diary of John Alden's reveals that he often wished that instead of joining Miles Standish in Duxbury he had Nahanted or even Saugused.

THE WRONGS OF SPRING
OR, NO ALL FOOLS' DAY LIKE
AN ALL OLD FOOLS' DAY

Just because I'm sixty-three,
Shall April folly forbidden be?
Though the locks above my scalp
Be thin as snow on August Alp,
Must I then leave April foibles
To sprouts of louts and hobbledehoibles?
I still remain the out-to-win type,
And I reply, "Not on your tintype!"
I will find a zany zebra,
I will teach the beast algebra;
Buy a Peugeot or a Simca,
Present it to a worthy YMCA;
Seek me out a sporting bishop,
Fit him with slaloms from a ski shop;
Roam through Perth and other Amboys,
Gathering luscious fraises and framboise,

To feast on with meringues and Nesselrodes
The while I drink a toast to Cecil Rhodes.
I'll write to some forlorn Penelope,
"S(ealed) W(ith) A K(iss)" on the envelope;
I'll memorize the works of Euripides
And match the footwork of centipedes.
I'll turn my mind to projects grandiose —
Regal, imperial, Ozymandiose —
Be Orientally lethargical,
Sybaritic, Maharajical,
And write, while lolling in my tub,
A syllabus on syllabub.
So I'll pace out my seven ages
By various frolicsome ambages —
A word that means, in Webster's phrase,
By roundabout or winding ways.
Thus, when April hoots her girlish laughter
My senile cackle shall echo after.

ROLL ON, THOU DEEP AND
DARK BLUE SYLLABLES,
ROLL ON

Like Stephen Vincent Benét, I have fallen in love with
American names;
Indeed, I even go so far as to call our own Tems the Thames.
Why, then, am I saddened by the appearance of so many
American names on the roster of the Metropolitan
Opera?
Well, not because I am as flighty as a butterfly, flutteriest
member of the order of Lepidopera.
No, it is because of my affection for the gentle dean of opera
commentators, Milton Cross,
Without whose sonorous Saturday synopses my radio during
the singing season would be a total loss.
Here is the ultimate interpreter of a libretto,
A man who can get two "*r*'s" and three "*t*'s" into his pro-
nunciation of "Rigoletto,"
A host both knowledgeable and suave,
Impeccable in his differentiation between the Italian "*c*"
and double "*c*" as in his virtuosity with German "*achs*"
and umlauts, and French nasals and accents both *aigus*
and *graves*.
He savors each name like a vintage rare and mellow;
I love to taste with him such delectabilities as Loretta Di
Franco, Raina Kabaivanska, Gabriella Tucci, Biserka
Cvejic, Gabor Carelli, Pekka Nuotio, Arturo Sergi,
Anselmo Colzani, Mario Sereni, Tito Gobbi, Elfego
Esparza, Cesare Siepi, Giorgio Tozzi, and Ezio Flagello.
I adore with him the exotic bouquet of other labels that the
Metropolitan cellars have a prodigious store of,

Such as Ludmila Dvorakova, Lili Chookasian, Ruza Po-
    spinov, Gaetano Bardini, Carlo Bergonzi, Flaviano
    Labò, Bonaldo Giaiotti, and, of course, Nicola
    Ghiuselev and Nicolai Ghiaurov.
An easy chair, an open fire, a radio tuned to an opera with
    a cast of foreign artists, and Maestro Cross in there
    really giving —
Boy, that's living!
But, O Beverly Bower, O Phyllis Curtin, O Grace Bumbry,
    Jean Fenn, Laurel Hurley, Shirley Love, Nell Rankin,
    Nancy Williams, and Evelyn Lear,
I grant that each of you is a delight to hear,
And O James King, Jess Thomas, William Walker, Robert
    Merrill, Richard Tucker, William Dooley, George Lon-
    don, Jerome Hines, and Norman Scott,
I grant that each of you is an artiste supreme — but names
    worthy of my idol's talents you have not!
O Rudolf Bing,
When casting, remember one thing:
None does more than Milton can
To justify the Met to man.

PAPERBACK, WHO MADE THEE? DOST THOU KNOW WHO MADE THEE?

A question that bothers me a lot
Is that of who invented what.
The Russians, as is widely known,
Were first to devise the telephone,
The electric toothbrush and Yorkshire pudding
And universal brotherhooding,
And motels and middle-income flats
And polyunsaturated fats,
Yet with all modesty they deny
Invention of the Great Big Lie,
And they are curiously lax
In claiming the credit for paperbacks.
I've often wondered what kindly gnomes
Originated these useful tomes.
I therefore gratefully shook the hand
Of a traveler from an antique land.
He told me a tale you may think is tall,
But it settled the matter once and for all.
Deep in the sand, in a bricked-up hole,
He had come across an authentic scroll
In which an Egyptian gave his version
Of a conversation with a Persian.
It occurred many thousand years ago
Where crocodiles lurk and lotuses grow.
Hotep asked with courtesy stately,
"Been reading any good pyramids lately?
Cheops's new one is simply terrific,
He cuts an absorbing hieroglyphic."
"I can't afford it," answered Cyrus back,
"I'm waiting until it's out in papyrus-back."

[29]

HARK, HARK,
THE LARKS DO BARK

Every schoolboy knows a wallaby from a wombat,
But only bright schoolboys know that the lark fight and not
the dog fight is the most personal form of aerial combat.
Take the duel between those two rivals for the heart of a
frivolous lady lark who to each had beckoned:
Percy B. Shelley's lark and the lark celebrated in *Sound of
Music* by Oscar Hammerstein II.
The Shelley lark was from heaven or near it amorously pour-
ing its full heart,
And the comments of the Hammerstein lark were jealous
and tart.
Its very salutation was pert:
"Hail to thee, whatever thou mayst be, because it's on record
that bird thou never wert.
Thou wert never even a gnatcatcher or a goatsucker or a
godwit or yet a skua bird."
And the Shelley lark said, "I am too a bird!"
And the Hammerstein lark said, "I will argue to and fro not,
Shelley himself admits that what thou art we know not.
He said that maybe thou wast a highborn maiden in a palace
tower, or perhaps a glowworm golden in a bed of dew.
Does that sound like a bird to you?"
And the Shelley lark said, "Shelley says, what says Shelley,
let Shelley say!
What says Oscar Hammerstein II? He says only that you are
still learning to pray.
A fine claim you have to be famous!

[30]

At your age I not only knew all of 'Now I Lay Me,' but also I
    could whistle 'Lead Kindly Light' and 'Venite Adore-
    mus.' "
Here the lady lark, who had been yawning, exclaimed, "Oh,
    skip it!"
And went off with a tone-deaf pipit.

ANY FULL NAME
IS A GRAND OLD NAME

Time and time again I've erred,
Turned from pew to peccadillo;
Many a sorry deed and word
Haunts me as I seek my pillow.
Though I struggle but in vain
Against my all too human nature
I yet have managed to maintain
Respect for human nomenclature.

If I overcompensate
In my flight from prunes and prisms
And perversely deviate
Into horrid solecisms,
Though my hearers I've appalled
With "Okey-doke" and "All the samey,"
Never, never have I called
Mrs. Eisenhower Mamie.

Mention gluttony and sloth,
Sins as profitless as deadly,
Often I've indulged in both,
And even in a graver medley,

Yet I swear that not for me
Lingo of the lout and lackey;
On my lips she'll always be
Mrs. Kennedy, not Jackie.

I've never called a sovereign Liz
To prove that I'm better than her equal;
That Meg to me a Margaret is
Can only be the natural sequel.
Coarse of tongue though I may be,
Witless, wearisome and windy,
He's Mr. President to me,
Not Lucky Lyndy.

AND SO MANHATTAN
BECAME AN ISLE OF JOY

I do not know the name of the last chief of the Manhattan
Indians, to me he is anonymous,

I suppose he had a name somewhere between the Pow-
hatanish and the Sitting Bullish or the Geronimous.

I am sure, however, that his life followed the familiar pat-
tern,

And that after three consecutive summers in which he had
not been able to get out of town he was thoroughly
sick of Manhattan.

He said that he was not just suffering from the nostalgia that
senescence often brings,

But that people didn't use to go around digging up the trails
to locate lost or hidden springs;

People, he said, to whom digging was undoubtedly some
form of drug,

Because as soon as they filled in a hole they apologized and
  started digging again just where they had previously
  dug.
He said that the spreading tepees had crowded out the
  beavers and mooses,
And that he didn't feel safe on the trails after dark because
  of the delinquent papooses.
Manhattan, he said, was going to the bowwows,
The average brave and squaw simply couldn't afford the
  ridiculous number of scalps demanded for admission to
  any of the ten top powwows.
He said that although by the medicine men air pollution
  was strictly forbidden,
Yet the continuous fall of ashes from illegal smoke signals
  left his lungs feeling like the tribal refuse dump, or
  midden.
To his untutored mind, he said, life in Manhattan was so
  unpleasant that he didn't care to continue it,
So he sold the place for twenty-four dollars to Peter Minuit.
Do you know what he said when he found he had been
  hornswoggled? I will tell you what he said:
Boy, is my face red!

THE ARMCHAIR GOLFER
OR, WHIMPERS OF A
SHORTCHANGED VIEWER

It's thirty-five miles from Chesapeake Bay,
A hundred from Cape Henlopen,
But it's also here on my old TV,
The site of the U.S. Open.

The gallery sways like a primitive throng
At a ceremony pagan,
And murmurs the names of its ancient gods,
Ouimet and Jones and Hagen.

Then swirls around the gods of today
An argumentative chorus:
Can Player match muscle with Nicklaus?
Can Palmer give weight to Boros?

We must wait, my friend, till the drama's end
Unfolds on the magic screen,
So join me here at my nineteenth hole
While they play the first fourteen.

The mysterious first fourteen, my friend,
Which is missing on my screen;
At times I wonder if anyone plays
The invisible first fourteen.

That the Open crown is a kingly crown
Is a statement we all endorse,
But I can't conceal that I sometimes feel
It is won on a four-hole course.

[34]

At times I think they have rolled the dice
To decide what their scores will be
As they swing a club for the very first time
When they stand on the fifteenth tee.

But hush! The sponsor is speaking now
The first commercial unrolls
And you settle yourself in your easy chair
To follow the last four holes.

Well, two-ninths of a loaf is better than none
And the picture is sharp and clean;
Just be grateful you're there for the final four,
And the hell with the first fourteen.

FABLES BULFINCH FORGOT:
NARCISSUS AND THE
TREACHEROUS VOWEL

I believe that people before they graduate or even matricu-
     late,
They should learn to speak up, to speak out, to articulate.
It befuddles my sense acoustic
To be mumbled at through a potato, be it from Idaho or
     Aroostook.
This word-swallowing, these muffled mutes and slovenly
     slurrings
Can lead to calamitous misunderstandings and errings.
Consider Narcissus, the irony of whose fate would give a
     Schopenhauer sardonicus risus.
To begin with, he was sired by one of three rivers all of
     whom were named Cephisus.

Narcissus after an insecure infancy escalated to manhood
and encountered a slender sylph he thought sublime,
And he kept talking about her all the time.
He himself was loved by Echo,
But he spurned her advances because she kept referring to
him as El Greco.
He was slipshod about his vowels, they came out thick
where they should have been thin,
His speech was related to that of the Joplin maiden on a
cruise who doesn't ask the number of other maidens
aboard, she just wants to know how minny min.
This habit betrayed him into a how-do-you-do as pretty as
any in that deviationist satire, *The Little Golden Calf*,
by Yevgeny Petrov and Ilya Ilf,
Because Echo, whom he had jilted, told everyone that he
was going around saying, "Oh how I love myself," when
he was really saying, "Oh how I love my sylph."
As a result, his name has become a synonym for egotistic;
Indeed, I have even heard him called Narcissistic.
The moral may be read between the lines of Ovid and of
Aesop:
Intelligible speech is not necessarily the mark of the milk-
sop or the teasop.
It's easy to be manly and still make your meaning plain,
whether in accents of Mount Ida, or Boston, of Des
Moines or of the deepest South;
Just take that towel out of your mouth.

NO BUSKIN, ALL SOCK,
MAKES LAUGHINGSTOCK

I tell the solemn tale of one
Foredoomed to be a figure of fun,
In youth debarred from one-o-cat
Unless he furnished ball and bat.
At forty he lost his thinning locks,
At fifty he caught chicken-pox.
His days with insults were infested,
His tailor called him pigeon-chested,
His fellow-workers called him Stupe,
His blood was of the commonest group,
And if to dance he ever chose,
The lady left to powder her nose.
His mouth was where he kept his foot,
His wife had with him up to put.
At table once he sulked and frowned
At meat the butcher man had ground.
She said with glance that spoke a tome
She'd gladly grind the meat at home
If he'd eliminate, by himself,
The mouse that roamed the pantry shelf.
Declaring naught would suit him more,
He hurried to the hardware store.
He said he'd like a mousetrap, please,
With warranties and guarantees,
Then added, needing no reminder,
Also their costliest meat-grinder.
The hardware man exclaimed, perplexed,
"What diet will they think of next?"

SONGLAND REVISITED
OR, THERE'S NO PURITY LIKE IMMATURITY

Songland has one characteristic in common with the
  Western of TV and cinema;
Black is black and white is white and intermediate colors
  are reduced to their minima.
In God's country you can tell the Bad Guys from the Good
  Guys by their complexions and leers;
In Songland, the distinguishing feature is simply years.
In the Western you can put your trust in non-swarthy non-
  leering alcoholic old doctors and sympathetic sheriffs;
And in Songland virtue is totally restricted to a host of
  happy adolescent but nubile seraphs.
By junior citizens only are worn the halos and the laurels;
In Songland it's a long long way from May even to July,
  and crabbed age and youth are poles apart not only
  in years but in morals.
Boys are good and Girls are good and their relationships are
  blissful and blameless,
But the conduct of Men (a pejorative) and Women (an-
  other pejorative) is consistently shameless.
The Men and Women of Songland are given to infidelity,
  sadism, intoxication, flagellation, desertion, homicide,
  and mopery,
Indeed a truly unsavory *potpourri.*
Look at the Man who done Frankie wrong, look at My Man,
  look at Old Man River, and that St. Louis Woman, do
  you think the Decalogue contains one commandment
  they took any heed of?
Look at the Moaner of Moanin' Low, what kind of a woman
  must she have been whom the kind of a man like him
  she moaned for stood in need of?

Such is the fiat laid down by Songland's muse;
Ballads are strictly reserved for the Boys and Girls, Men
and Women only get to get into the blues.
Well, who am I to carp at the plan divine?
As long as you're up, pass me a beaker of that good young
Boy Oh Boyischewitz wine.

SPLINTERS FROM THE FESTIVE BOARD

TASTE BUDS, EN GARDE!

Although I'll eat the strawberry when frozen
It's not the very berry I'd have chosen.
The naughty admen claim with gall divine
That it is better than the genu-ine,
New language they devise to sing its praise,
But only *le bon Dieu* can coin a *fraise*.

ONE WESTERN, TO GO

I know a lady, name of Blanche,
Who roughed it smoothly on a ranch,
Digesting in her cowpoke garb
Flapjacks and beans without bicarb,
And urging in raucous campfire song
The little dogie to git along.
She spoke a blend of gin and vamoose,
Confusing coyote with cayuse,
But never her buxom self entrusted
Save to a bronco thoroughly busted.
"Though *The Virginian* I have read,
I'm just a tenderloin," she said.

EXPERIMENT DEGUSTATORY

A gourmet challenged me to eat
A tiny bit of rattlesnake meat,
Remarking, "Don't look horror-stricken,
You'll find it tastes a lot like chicken."
It did.
Now chicken I cannot eat.
Because it tastes like rattlesnake meat.

AVANTI, GOURMETTI!

Sea horses may be Romanized
By calling them hippocampi;
If you would do the same to shrimp,
Add garlic, and they're scampi.

THE PIONEER

I seek in anonymity's cloister
Not him who ate the first raw oyster,
But one who, braving spikes and prickles,
The spine that stabs, the leaf that tickles,
With infinite patience and fortitude
Unveiled the artichoke as food.

EVERYBODY'S FULL OF CARBONACEOUS MATERIAL OBTAINED BY THE IMPERFECT COMBUSTION OF WOOD

That cigarette you lately puffed,
Its filter was with charcoal stuffed.
The vodka in your Bloody Mary
Seeped through charcoal ubiquitary.
Regard your lobsters or your steaks,

They're black with crispy charcoal flakes.
Let it be writ on history's page
We're living in a charcoal age;
Those pangs you feel are not gastritis,
You're suffering, friend, from charcolitis.

THE SHORT ORDER COCKTAIL
OR, ONE COOK TO TAKE OUT

Once there was a couple named Mr. and Mrs. Plackett,

And for many years they had more domestic helpers than any of their friends of similar status and bracket.

They had had a whole alphabet of helpers, from Agatha and Adelaide right through Karen and Katinka all the way to Yolanda and Zenobia,

And Mrs. Plackett was happy, because the very thought of cooking or washing up inspired a feverish phobia.

Mr. Plackett was happy for Mrs. Plackett but somewhat given to self-pity,

Because the evening meal was invariably set before him twenty minutes after he got home from the city,

And he barely had time to wash up, much less settle down quietly to a second martini or old-fashioned,

And he felt he was being arbitrarily rationed,

But if he didn't like it he could go stand in the nearest breadline,

Because Agatha or Katinka or whoever it was that week had an inviolable bus-catching deadline.

One night Mr. Plackett came home to find his wife broken-hearted,

Because the most recent domestic engineer had worked herself into a huff over some fancied slight and summarily departed,

And the episode wasn't laughable, it was wailable,

Because the employment agency reported that there were
no more domestic engineers available.
Mr. Plackett didn't wail, but he knew enough not to laugh,
And he said, Well, dear, let's ponder the situation over a
companionable drink and then have a pickup supper
of canned soup and toast and canned peaches and in-
stant coffee in about an hour and a half.
He was as comforting as he was able,
But all the time he was thinking that now he could finish
his cocktail at his leisure instead of either gulping it
down or carrying it with him to the table.
His heart leaped up at the prospect of sit-down-when-you-
are-darned-good-and-ready dining,
But he considered it wise to make sure that Mrs. Plackett
caught some glimpse of silver lining,
And she gradually began to stop weeping like a willow
When he said, Do you remember how They used to leave
strange parts of the vacuum cleaner on the living-room
sofa and damp cleaning rags drying on top of my
pillow?
And she smiled through her tears and said she also remem-
bered how he had nobly refrained from mayhem and
slaughter
Those many times when he had gone to the refrigerator for
more ice and discovered that They had forgotten to
refill the ice trays with water.
Mr. Plackett's self-confidence now grew more hearty;
He reminded her how They inevitably came up with the
funeral of a dear one just the morning before she had
planned something special in the way of a party.
By now she was giggling deliciously,
And she reminded him how whenever They were around,
the level in the bourbon bottle kept dwindling sus-
piciously,

And he said yes, he was a battle-scarred campaigner

And had grown to regard any one of them who stayed long enough to get really high as a faithful old family retainer.

His second cocktail he then began to quaff,

And on him was the last laugh,

Because he hadn't noticed that during their conversation Mrs. Plackett had been darting in and out of the room like Fanny Farmer on a spree,

And five minutes earlier than the usual hour she curtsied archly and announced, *Monsieur est servi.*

Mr. Plackett emptied his glass into a vase of petunias and called on Heaven for aid,

And every evening thereafter when he got home he read the evening paper over a couple of indolently sipped cocktails and then took his wife out for dinner, either at Joe's Place or Chez Marcel, depending on how things had gone that day in the marts of trade.

THE UNIQUENESS OF
MR. ONATIVIA

England has long been noted for its crop of notable eccentrics,

So I am happy to present one American who rivals such gentry in their gentricks.

Shake hands with Mr. Onativia,

Who because the world is so full of a number of horrendous things devotes his mind exclusively to trivia.

He does not lie awake worrying about whether Soviet antimissile devices can frustrate our Polaris,

He is too busy insisting that singers sing "June Is Bustin'
Out All Over" only in June and "April in Paris" not only
only in April but also only in Paris.

He holds that anyone but a lovesick Ubangi who sings "The
Shadow of Your Smile" is with the facts of physiognomy
playing loose and fast,

Because by whose smile except a Ubangi maiden's can a
shadow be cast?

Mr. Onativia is originator of the Onativia Plan,

In which he has pledged assistance to all who object to the
locution "different than."

With followers of Bergen Evans his approach is teasing
rather than harsh;

He simply asks them if they know the difference than a
tournedos and a tornado, the difference than a Jacobin
and a Jacobite, or the difference than a détente and a
démarche.

You can see that Mr. Onativia is not given to the crude
exhibitionism that Eighteenth Century squires were
wont to practice,

But I think his mild eccentricities nicer than jumping your
horse over the dining room table and growing coarse
and red-faced on a diet of claret and roast beef *au jus
primae noctis.*

THE MOOSE ON THE BEACH

Old Daddy Slipper-Slopper jumped out of bed,
He opened the window and he poked out his head,
Mumbling and mouthing,
"The wild geese are southing,
And a moose is loose on the beach."

Bob went his head and pop went his eyes
At the moose on the beach and the geese in the skies,
Three wavering strings
Of unwavering wings
As loose as the moose on the beach.

The gaggle flew stragglewise above the sea,
They couldn't remember how to form a V.
Three leaders at their chore
Were even more
Obtuse than the moose on the beach.

The three strings strayed a-sprawl and a-spraddle,
They merged and parted like a silly cat's cradle,
You could almost believe
They were trying to weave
A noose for the moose on the beach.

Then the leaders honked in the salty breeze
And the geese disappeared as three great V's,
Three V's that sped
Over Great Boar's Head,
And the deuce with the moose on the beach.

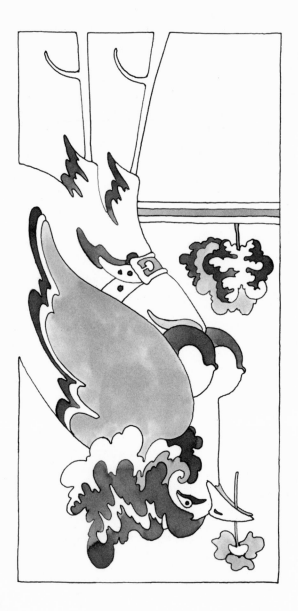

WHO CALLED THAT
PIED-BILLED GREBE A
PODILYMBUS PODICEPS
PODICEPS?

All I know about the bird:
It is feathered, not furred.
Ornithologists know all about the bird,
But their nomenclature is absurd.
As scientists, they are naturally pedantic,
But they are also afflicted with a compulsion to repetition
    that is hysterical and frantic.
Their needle is caught in a groove, a cog is missing in their
    pianola,
Hence we find the black-bellied plover turning up as
    Squatarola squatarola.
We laymen are not so woolly-minded as they think us —
We get the point when they call a mallard *Anas platyrhyn-
    chos;* they need not belabor it by proceeding to *Anas
    platyrhynchos platyrhynchos.*
Their bubbling bibble-babble is truly splendiferous;
Think upon the redheaded woodpecker, or *Melanerpes
    erythrocephalus erythrocephalus,* as well as the killdeer,
    or *Charadrius vociferus vociferus.*
Stay me with parsnips, comfort me with sarsaparilla —
From the pine siskin they have hatched a *Spinus pinus pinus*
    and from the eastern field sparrow a *Spizella pusilla
    pusilla.*
(And in parenthis,
While speaking of sparrows, what meagre meal is com-
    memorated by terming the savanna sparrow *Passerculus
    sandwichensis?*)

Did Little Sir Echo originate the double- and triple-headed
 terminology they stuff in us?
How else did the eastern harlequin duck become *Histrioni-
 cus histrionicus* and the Manx shearwater turn into
 Puffinus puffinus puffinus?
By Allah,
I believe all ornithologists must be natives of Pago Pago,
 Baden Baden, or Walla Walla.

HOW PLEASANT TO
APE MR. LEAR

A crusader's wife slipped from the garrison
And had an affair with a Saracen.
    She was not oversexed,
    Or jealous or vexed,
She just wanted to make a comparison.

A novelist of the absurd
Has a voice that will shortly be heard.
    I learn from my spies
    He's about to devise
An unprintable three-letter word.

The Pilgrims ate quahaugs and corn yet,
Which gourmets would scorn through a lorgnette.
    For this kind of living
    They proclaimed a Thanksgiving.
I'm thankful I hadn't been born yet.

An exiled Iraqi went back
To his home with a ewe in his pack.
    He said people all knew
    Every Q needs a U
So he put the ewe back in Iraqu.

In Duluth there's a hostess, forsooth,
Who doesn't know gin from vermouth,
    But this lubricant lapse
    Isn't noticed, perhaps
Because nobody does in Duluth.

A Knight of the Garter long hence
Was expelled from that order of gents.
    He was fairly adroit
    When he cried "Honi Soit,"
But he couldn't pronounce "Mal y Pense."

A lama of Outer Mongolia
Was seized with acute melancholia.
    When the Chinese asked why
    He could only reply,
You'd chop off my head if I tolia.

There was a young girl of Milwaukee
Whose voice was sc-r-reechy and squawky.
    Her friends were emphatic
    It sounded like static
And called her their Milwaukee-talkie.

A chuckling tycoon of Fort Worth,
When asked for the cause of his mirth,
    Replied, Houston and Dallas
    Will shore bust a gallus
When they hear I've just purchased the earth.

Said a commissar loyal but vague,
"This changing of names is a plague!
    I was ordered by Og-
    pu to take over Prague,
And now I discover it's Prague!"
      (ED. NOTE: Ha ha,
          It's Praha!)

THE INDIGNANT OWL

My dear Mr. Lear, oh my dear Mr. Lear,
The moment has come for a flea in your ear.
I have heard your unflattering sequel to Homer
In which I'm described as an amorous roamer,
The most lubberly bubble-head skipper afloat
With a *faute de mew* crew in a honey-smeared boat,
In which, to top off your fantastic narration,
You baldly accuse me of miscegenation.
In forest or meadow or green arboretum
Pussycats I don't woo, sir, preferring to eatum.
I'm an owl, I'm an owl, I am ominous-eyed,
I'm Athena's preceptor, the Parthenon's pride.
I am old, I am wise, and I slay when I swoop,
I could rake off your beard in one iron-clawed scoop.
You were known as a great ornithologist once;
As an owl man you're proven a runcible dunce.
Your effusion has filled me with cold collywobbles;
Please return, Mr. Lear, to your Jumblies and Pobbles.

A thrifty soprano of Hingham
Designed her own dresses of gingham.
On the blue and white squares
She wrote opera airs
So when they wore out she could singham.

A male entomologist author
Waxed wrother and wrother and wrother —
He socked his own brother
Who called him a mother
Instead of an eminent mother.

There was a young man from New Haven
Who loved Shakespeare, from Stratford-on-Avon.
He claimed that the bard,
Besides plays by the yard,
Wrote *Paradise Lost* and *The Raven*.

I admire St. Simeon Stylites,
Who, faced with a shortage of nighties,
Sanctimonious and solemn,
Reached up from his column
And quietly pinched the Almighty's.

An old Danish jester named Yorick
Drank a gallon of pure paregoric.
My jokes have been dull,
Said he, but my skull
Will one of these days be historic.

There once was an umpire whose vision
Was cause for abuse and derision.
    He remarked in surprise,
    Why pick on my eyes?
It's my heart that dictates my decision.

How the Avant-Garde loves to annoy
The gullible gaping *polloi*.
    Soon some underground flicker
    Will prove with a snicker
That Helen of Troy was a boy.

A princess who lived near a bog
Met a prince in the form of a frog.
    Now she and her prince
    Are the parents of quints,
Four boys and one fine polliwog.

A handsome young rodent named Gratian
As a lifeguard became a sensation.
    All the lady mice waved
    And screamed to be saved
By his mouse-to-mouse resuscitation.

A co-ed protester named Lil
Cried, "Those C.I.A. squares make me ill!
    First they bugged our martinis,
    Our bras and bikinis,
And now they are bugging The Pill."

SONGS OF EXPERIENCE

IF A BODER MEET A BODER,
NEED A BODER CRY? YES.

I haven't much faith in bodings; I think that all bodings are
daft bodings.

Forebodings are bad enough, but deliver me from aft-
bodings.

Aftbodings are what too many of us suffer from subsequent
to making decisions even of the most inconsequential
and niggling.

Aftbodings prevent people in restaurants from enjoying
their haunch of venison, because they keep wondering
if they shouldn't have ordered the roast crackling suck-
ling pigling.

Aftbodings are what women are constantly up to their
midriffs amid,

Because they are always afraid that the hats or dresses
they didn't buy are more becoming than the ones they
did.

Aftbodings trouble the young executive who has opted for
a martini instead of a bloody mary, and plague the
rascally artist who too late feels that he should have
forged that Gainsborough instead of this Romney.

Aftbodings are the major cause of insomny.

Consider the lines "Of all sad words . . . the saddest are
these: 'It might have been!' " whittled by J. G. Whittier;

As an example of aftboding, what could be prettier?

Indeed, I deem this an example of aftboding *in excelsis,*

Because J. G. Whittier wasn't even boding after his own
decision but somebody else's.

I myself am more and more inclined to agree with Omar and
with Satchel Paige as I grow older:

Don't try to rewrite what the moving finger has writ, and
don't ever look over your shoulder.

ILL-MET BY FLUORESCENCE
OR, EVERYBODY'S DOING IT WHO'D
RATHER BE ESCHEWING IT

I know a dance, a perilous dance,
A demoniac duet,
It's a ritual now habitual
With the older married set.
It's danced in seven-room co-op
And ivied ranch-style cot,
It's that conjugal collidoscope
The Bottleneck Gavotte.

What celibate pseudo-architect,
What very prince of asses,
Built such complex of bottlenecks,
Such network of impasses?
Now man and wife 'twixt bed and bath,
Or oven and china-shelf,
In kitchen door, at bureau drawer,
Forever meet themself.

Advance and bump, retreat, repeat,
With many a sparkling glance,
It's eye to eye and rump to thigh —
So goes the intricate dance.
She raises the soup above her head
While he props door with knee,
He steps to left and she to right,
And again they're vis-à-vis.

He sidles thus, she sidles so,
In movements contrapuntal,

He backs, she fills, they stand transfixed
In permanent confrontal.
Oh, there's many a couple with bumpers hooked
Like cars in a parking lot,
Frozen as on a Grecian urn
In the Bottleneck Gavotte.

WHILE HOMER NODDED:
A FOOTNOTE TO THE ILIAD

In the days when the hollow ships of the well-greaved Achaeans were beached off Priam's city there was a two-faced Achaean named Antiscrupulos,

And he was so two-faced that his duplicity was doubled, it was quadrupulous.

He was owner of a mighty fleet which was not under Achaean registry, it flew the flag of the Hesperides,

And his ships were never hollow, they were always full of costly cargoes such as maidens available for sacrifice, and lotus, the predecessor of L.S.D., and cantharides.

He was far too busy to spend any time hurling insults at Hector on the ringing plains of windy Troy,

He was always furrowing the wine-dark sea in search of costlier cargoes, and nearly always accompanied by a fascinating hetaera, which was the contemporary term for a daughter of joy.

But once he didn't take her with him and he got home a day early and what did he behold?

There was his hetaera in a compromising situation with a shower of gold,

And he said, How do you excuse such misconduct? and she said, I don't need any excuse,

This isn't really a shower of gold, it's aegis-bearing Zeus.

Well, Antiscrupulos was very moral about other people's
morals, anent which he was a veritable bluenose,

And he was also jealous as a dozen Heras or Junos,

So after precautiously sacrificing a surplus maiden to aegis-
bearing Zeus he accused aegis-bearing Zeus of being
a compulsive seducer and a menace to Achaean woman-
hood both mortal and immortal,

And Zeus did not incinerate him with a thunderbolt, he just
gave a thunderous self-satisfied lecherous chortle.

Antiscrupulos grew even more indignant and ventured on
further prods,

He said, How can you chortle off your licentious behavior,
you who should set an example of marital fidelity for
us humans, you who bear the dread responsibility of
being monarch of Olympus and king of all the gods?

He said, Tell me, O king of all the gods, for your godless
philandering can you offer the shadow of an excuse,
the ghost of an excuse, the wraith of an excuse, even
the wraithiest?

And Zeus said, Yes, I'm an atheist.

CHANT AT THE END OF
A BEGINNINGLESS SUMMER

The sky is overcast and I am undercast and the fog creeps
in on little iceberg feet,

And there is no retreat.

I would don my Job-like false whiskers and my straggly
King Lear wig;

I shake them, and out drops an earwig.

Oh dank, dank, dank, there is no chill in the martini nor
warmth in the toddy,

The aura of the house is that of a damp demd moist unpleasant body.
You will note that I cannot even quote Dickens correctly, as once I used,
In this weather all my Dickens have gone back to Proust.
In this weather, in this weather
One hundred six-cent stamps and fifty air-mails have become permanently glued together.
At night eaves drip and foghorn moans in tuneless timeless antiphony,
I have not seen the moon since the second Sunday after Epiphany.
Strangely, I find I miss the moon no whit,
Nor have I since the two U.S.'s have changed her from "she" to "it."
I want to return to the womb,
No matter of whom.
Respect my gloom, my gloom is lodged in my craw,
Do not mark, fold, tear or staple my gloom, it is recommended for mature audiences, it is void where prohibited by law.
Summer that never was, of seeing yoursel as others see ye I'll gie ye the giftie;
No maiden of bashful fifteen like other summers hae ye been, but unco like, as Richard Brinsley Sheridan almost said,
A weirdo of fifty.

ADMONITORY LINES FOR THE BIRTHDAY OF AN OVER-ENERGETIC CONTEMPORARY

Lord, the calendar is droll;
How the years more rapid roll!
How the candles on the cake
By some ludicrous mistake
Seem to increase at every session
In geometrical progression!
I've noticed as their numbers mount
That you, old friend, forget to count,
So as the final flame you blow on
I make a wish for you to grow on.
May angels watch o'er your well-being
And turn your thoughts away from skiing,
Preserve your venturesome soul from lusting
For surfing or for bronco-busting,
From stalking grizzlies with bow and arrow
Or climbing up Mount Kilimanjaro,
Or, seeking novelty, to begin
Diving, either sky- or skin-,
And if you find you can't resist
Frug and other forms of twist
To shield with heavenly umbrella
Sacroiliac and patella,
And when the sun with Sunday mingles
Steer you to doubles instead of singles;
Then with these perils all behind
To keep you ever young of mind,
Give that most generous of hearts
Compassion for the current arts.

Be patient facing the jejunest
Pontificating Popportunist,
Don't bridle at Genet or Albee,
Admit that much that was not shall be.
So future anniversary binges
Will find no twinges in your hinges.
And now this placid five-toed sloth
Concludes by crying, God bless us both!

LITTLE PRETTY PENNY,
LET'S SQUANDER THEE

Why do so many billionaires go in for penuriousness
Instead of luxuriousness?
Why are so many prosperous potential sybarites
Afraid of being termed flibbertigibberites?
Too many tycoons who would relish a display of extra-
vagance
Explore the edges of ostentation in a sort of timid cir-
cumnavigance.
If I were Mr. Onassis do you know what I would do? I
would buy Neiman-Marcus
And give it for Easter to Mr. Niarchos.
If I were Mr. Niarchos I might buy the Parthenon
And present it to the Huntington Hartford Museum after
changing its name to the General MacArthurnon.
Were I the favorite customer of Harry Winston
I might well acquire the Green Bay Packers and give them
to Rutgers for use in the game with Princeton,
Or were I a Nizam counting my rubies and emeralds and
wives in my Oriental palace
I'd find it a change of pace to present Dallas to Madame
Callas, or even Madame Callas to Dallas.

[68]

Were I an Aga or a Khan fond of a friend despite his gross addiction to food and drink who might therefore be described as crapulous,

I would give him a deed to Le Pavillon and Lüchow's and La Tour d'Argent and all the Indian pudding in Indianapulous.

I'd like to say to a Gulbenkian or a Rockefeller, why don't you show in what league you are?

Why don't you transport the Taj Mahal and use it as a guesthouse in Antigua?

Had I the wells of an **H**. L. Hunt I would be openhanded like Cardinal Wolsey, not close-fisted like Cardinal Mazarin,

I would raise and refit the Andrea Doria just for a cruise around Manhattan Island and set before my guests a feast Lucullan, yea, even Belshazzaran.

Upon arising next noon I would taper on to prodigality again by making the kind of humble propitiatory offering that Midas might have made to Zeus or Hera,

I would spend a modest $1700 on an appropriate gift for President de Gaulle, an item advertised by a Park Avenue shop consisting of a limestone fossil fish plaque 60 million years old, a relic of the Eocene Era.

I would also, may my tribe increase,

Present every taxi-driver in New York with a lifetime supply of cigars costing not less than a dollar apiece.

Whether glory or infamy would be my lot I know not which,

But I would surely carve for myself a special niche among the rich.

THE DARKEST HALF-HOUR
OR, TOO EARLY IS THE TIME FOR
ALL GOOD GUESTS TO COME TO
THE AID OF THE PARTY

They are ready for their party.

He feels as elegant as the Sun King and she as divine as
the Moon Goddess, Astarte.

They have asked the guests for 7:30 on this, they hope,
effulgent eve,

And by 7:05 they are in the living room, poised, braced,
anticipatory, and on the *qui vive.*

Eagerly they await the doorbell, or, in certain climes,

The ripple of those melodious Wistful Vista chimes.

He starts to light a cigarette, but she halts him with gestures
frenzied —

The ashtrays have just been cleansèd.

She starts to sit on the sofa, and he, the most impartial um-
pire who never umped,

Evens the count by reminding her that the sofa has just
been plumped.

Then she divides the olives by the number of guests and
hopes she has not been too frugal,

And wishes that the caviar were not the sticky reddish kind
but genuinely Belugal.

He nervously whistles a snatch from the *Peer Gynt Suite,*
by Grieg,

And wonders if his vodka — domestic, not Polish — is fit for
compounding a White Russian, an Orange Julius, a
Bog Fog, or a Palm Bay Intrigue.

By 7:25 she is pacing the floor and nibbling at her finger-
    nails, destroying the opalescent symmetry acquired at
    the afternoon manicure,
And he inquires, "Are you sure it was *this* Saturday and not
    next that you asked them for?" — a question not recom-
    mended as the ideal panic cure.
At 7:30 they are tense as mummers awaiting the rise of the
    curtain, and at 7:31 they have abandoned their mum-
    ming —
They are convinced that nobody is coming.
So he says how about a quick one, and just as he has one
    hand in the ice bucket and the other on the gin,
Why, the first couple walks in.
You will be glad to learn that the party turned out to be
    absolutely fabulous;
Indeed, some say the best since the one at which a horse
    was named consul by the late Emperor Heliogabulus.

NOTES FOR THE CHART IN 306

The bubbles soar and die in the sterile bottle
Hanging upside down on the bedside lamppost.
Food and drink
Seep quietly through the needle strapped to the hand.
The arm welcomes the sting of mosquito hypodermic —
Conveyor of morphia, the comforter.
Here's drowsiness, here's lassitude, here's nothingness,
Sedation *in excelsis.*
The clouded mind would stray into oblivion
But for the grackle-squawk of the box in the hall,
The insistent call for a faceless goblin horde
Of sorcerers, vivisectionists, body-snatchers.

Dr. Polyp is summoned,
Dr. Gobbo and Dr. Prodigy,
Dr. Tortoise, Dr. Sawdust, and Dr. Mary Poppins,
La belle dame sans merci.
Now it's Dr. Bandarlog and Dr. Bacteria,
And last of all, the terrifying one,
Dodger Thomas.
And there is no lock on the door.
On the third day, the goblins are driven off
To the operating room beneath the hill.
Dr. Vandeleur routs gibbering Bandarlog,
Bacteria flees before swarthy Dr. Bagderian.
Sawdust and Polyp yield to Saunders and Pollitt,
And it's Porter instead of Tortoise who knocks at the door.
He will test the blood, not drain it.
The eerie impostors are gone, all gone but one —
Dodger Thomas.
I know he is lurking somewhere in a shadow.
Dodger Thomas.
I've never met him, but old friends have.
I know his habit:
He enters without knocking.

MR. JUDD AND HIS SNAIL,
A SORRY TALE
OR, NEVER UNDERESTIMATE THE WISDOM
OF A SAGE OF THE AGES

I offer one small bit of advice that Billy Graham could write
    a whole column on:
Never ignore any bit of advice offered by King Solomon.
I call your attention to the case of Philander Judd.
His veins were distended with optimism and sporting blood.
His interest in racing was enormous,
But he was by nature nonconformous.
He was not one of those who set their horses or greyhounds
    whirling around the track to their hearts' content, or
    à gogo,
He said he knew that something fast could go fast, he was
    interested in how fast could something slow go.
He considered conventional races pallid and stale,
So his entire stable consisted of one thoroughbred gastropod,
    or snail.
The snail, of course, is a mollusk akin to the whelk and the
    slug, and, as is known to every gastropodist,
It moves complacently on one ventral muscular foot, to the
    bewilderment of every biped chiropodist.
Mr. Judd entered his snail in every kind of race but one, for
    which he refused to name it,
And that one was a claiming race, because he was afraid
    that somebody, perhaps a Gallic gourmet, might claim
    it.
His snail was beaten in December by a tortoise, so he
    dropped it down a couple of classes,

And in January it lost by eight lengths to a jug of molasses.
By now Mr. Judd was deeply indebted to his bookie,
But being an honorable man, he couldn't get out of town
or stoop to any other form of welsher's hookey.
At last he thought he saw a way to settle with his creditors;
He found the perfect spot for his snail, a race in which an
amoeba and a glacier were the other two competitors.
The amoeba posed a real threat, but from the glacier he did
not flinch;
He had clocked it for a full month, during which it had
moved only three-quarters of an inch.
Therefore, although he could not be certain to win the race,
He knew he had a sure thing to place.
Yes, that was what he happily reckoned,
And he bet his remaining roll on the snail for second.
Well, the amoeba outdistanced the snail and the snail out-
distanced the glacier, and then just at the finish line
something out of the ordinary occurred;
The amoeba split apart and finished one two, and the snail
ran third.
Mr. Judd had forgotten what Solomon once told the Queen
of Sheba:
Never trust an Egyptian or an amoeba.

YUM YUM, TAKE IT AWAY

Do you wonder why, when you sit down to eat, you start
    twisting in your chair and drumming on the table with
    your digits?
Because of dysphoria, which is a state of dissatisfaction,
    anxiety, restlessness, or the fidgets,
Which is caused by anticipation of dysphagia, or difficulty
    in swallowing,
Which is caused by two hazards of dining with friends to-
    day, namely, the following:
Hazard number one is the hostess who fancies herself as a
    gourmet, or should I say gourmette;
Hers is a table at which even between courses you first take
    out and then hastily put back your cigarette.
When does a housewife blossom into a Brillat-Savarin? I
    will tell you when;
It is when she has a newspaper or magazine clipping, a clove
    of garlic, and a Rock Cornish hen.
Herbs are another status symbol, so as you work your way
    through the tossed epicurean forage,
Why, you are supposed to detect and appreciate the differ-
    ence between the oregano and the saxifrage, and the
    chervil and the borage.
Frankly, I don't know whether I'd less rather eat them or
    guess them;
If these be Herbs, I'm willing for Herb to repossess them.
Hazard number two is no gourmet, she is the backbone of
    the economy in this land of the free;
This hostess serves nothing that isn't displayed wrapped in
    cellophane at the supermarket exactly as advertised on
    her TV.

Even before by the first mouthful your palate is mortified

You know you will be confronted with substances presliced, processed, tenderized, polyunsaturated, dehydrated, or fortified.

You are in an evil humor;

If, as Sir Winston has said, the good is the enemy of the best, so is the just-as-good the enemy of the bemused consumer.

This truth is so evident that even the advertiser will occasionally resort to it as a final expedient;

Witness the less expensive spread that is promoted as better than other less expensive spreads because it boasts of containing some of the more expensive spread as an ingredient.

You know your desire is foolhardy, it is the essence of foolhardihoodness,

But you desire to eat something that tastes like something, rather than something you are told will zestfully stimulate your taste buds with its mouth-watering goodness.

Which last is an eventuality not to be trifled with;

I heard of one consumer who consumed a product so mouth-watering that his taste buds got over-mouth-watered and grew to the size of chrysanthemums, which he was stifled with.

This is the only exception I can give

To the paradoxical rule that the more insipid and unappetizing our diet, the longer we seem to live.

ALL OF THE PLEASURE AND NONE OF THE RESPONSIBILITY? LEAVES FROM A GRANDFATHER'S SUMMER JOURNALS

AIRY, AIRY, QUITE CONTRARY

All winter they've been simply frantic
To wallow in their own Atlantic.
They've chattered shrill of how they crave
To plunge beneath the curling wave;
With pagan fervor they exalt
The feel of sand, the tang of salt.
Comes summer and they ride with glee
Hundreds of miles to reach the sea.
What then? The ocean is too cool;
They seek the nearest motel pool.

ONE TIMES ONE IS EIGHT

Either old magic or new math
Into our house has beat a path.
How else could Einstein or Diogenes
Explain an exploit of our progeny's?
While at the table with his ilk
A child upsets a glass of milk.
The glass held half a pint when filled,
And half a gallon when it spilled.

THEIR STOMACH IS BIGGER
THAN YOUR EYES

We must not irritation feel
When children gorge before the meal.
The reason why is manifest —
That's when they are the hungriest.

APPREHENSION

Whose child is this with sodden clothes
And sneezing fits and runny nose?
Its temperature is ninety-nine;
I only know if it were mine
A steaming tub I'd soak it in
And leave the rest to aspirin.
The child does not belong to me,
I'm just a scrupulous trustee,
So I must call the doctor in
Who'll grunt, and order aspirin.

THE GENTLEMAN LADY'S MAID

A treat which I consider mild
Is dressing an impatient child.
It proves impossible to insert
The child in socks or drawers or shirt.
The process baffles brain and brawn,
The socks will just go halfway on,
The drawers cut the child in two
And the shirt won't let the head get through.
It's presently clear that one can not
Force last month's clothes on this month's tot.

PROTOCOL

Conflict fills the dining room
Over who sits next to whom.
Cries of "You sat there last time!"
Interrupt the grace sublime.
Darned if this decrepit recorder
Can understand their pecking order.

GRANDPA IS ASHAMED

A child need not be very clever
To learn that "Later, dear" means "Never."

THE HORRORS

All winter long I lose my poise
At any kind of slamming noise.
The memory of an impact lingers —
A car door, and a child's fingers.

THE ROMANTIC AGE

This one is entering her teens,
Ripe for sentimental scenes,
Has picked a gangling unripe male,
Sees herself in bridal veil,
Presses lips and tosses head,
Declares she's not too young to wed,
Informs you pertly you forget
Romeo and Juliet.
Do not argue, do not shout;
Remind her how that one turned out.

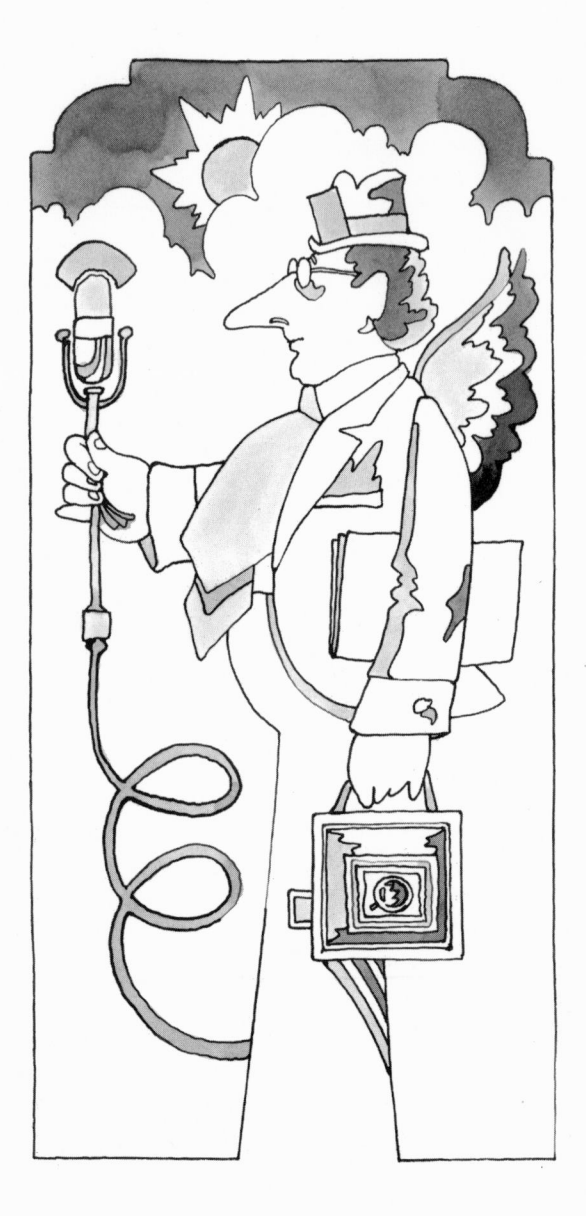

WHAT'S HECUBA TO HIM?
A ONE-MINUTE CLOSE-UP
OR, SOME NOSES FOR NEWS
ARE FOR TWEAKING

Once there was a TV Roving Reporter named Goucher
    Bumpus.

His nose for news was his compass.

His approach to his victims was sometimes hotly belligerent,

Sometimes cool as a refrigerant.

He had the manners of a hyena

And the persistence of a subpoena.

His questions were notable for their callosity

Because conscience never made a coward of him because he
    had no conscience, only curiosity.

His hand never trembled as he thrust the mike at the widow
    of a policeman or fireman killed on duty,

And his audio-video of the mother whose child had been
    run over was a thing of beauty.

At probing the emotions of relatives waiting for the casualty
    list at the airport he couldn't be bested,

And he had caused three murder convictions to be reversed
    because he had badgered confessions out of the ac-
    cused right after they were arrested.

He was indeed a worthy Roving Reporter,

And only on his arrival at Heaven's gate did he meet a
    worthy retorter.

No hagiolater he, he didn't bother to wheedle,

He bluntly demanded of the guardian if he honestly be-
    lieved that a million angels can dance on the point of a
    needle.

The result was ideal;

Many previous interviewees had told him where to go,
    but this time it was for real.

THE NONBIOGRAPHY OF
A NOBODY

There is one major compensation for being a minor literary
 figure,
Said Mr. Curmudgel, a minor literary figure.
Particularly, said Mr. Curmudgel,
A minor literary figure who
Has led a life bespectacled and unspectacular,
The kind of life, said Mr. Curmudgel,
The kind of life that Solomon Grundy lived,
Leaving behind no meat, just a white skeleton of dates.
Born, married, sickened, died and that's the lot.
There's little there for ghouls to feed on.
At least I know, said Mr. Curmudgel,
That when the reticent New Hampshire soil
Reluctant yields me one small oblong of nonbreathing space
There will be none to grind my bones to make their bread,
To speculate both on my sex and what strange uses
I may have made of it,
To snivel over my death wish drowned in alcohol or blood
 sports,
My secret gnawing envy of my peers,
To cram the public maw with spiteful hearsay
Authenticate only by vociferous claim to intimacy,
To friendship, good fellowship, and unique piquant revela-
 tions
Garnered over the rum pot.
Let me say once for all, said Mr. Curmudgel,
I was never a Golden Boy by self destroyed,
And the hairs on my chest at last count numbered three.

No spate of As I Knew Hims
Will lie like empty beer cans around my modest stone,
No carrion crows regurgitate juiceless shreds of me,
No middle-aged actors searching for the comeback trail
Clamor to cast their version of me on the screen.
Two inches or one in the *Times* and the printers are through
with me, I'll rest in peace,
A Solomon Grundy of American letters.
Solomon Grundy, said Mr. Curmudgel thoughtfully,
Married on Wednesday, took sick on Thursday, died on
Saturday.
By God, said Mr. Curmudgel,
Obviously an alcoholic with a death wish!
He slipped the cover from his dusty typewriter.

O TEMPORA, OH-OH!

The sober journal that I read
Reports the news discreetly;
When faced with carnal goings-on
It treads the tightrope featly.

It chronicles in dispassionate terms
Divorce and defloration,
And circumspectly drops its voice
To mention deviation.

No juicy tidbits does it toss
To those for thrills esurient —
Naught lickerish or snickerish
To gratify the prurient.

But oh, the Sunday Book Review!
I realize my stodginess
As children leaf it through with cries
Of "Daddy, what's erogenous?"

I'm grateful to the critics who
Submit for our advisements
Their résumés of current books —
But, boy, the advertisements!

Read all about that cultured cad
De Sade and his diversions,
Or sexual practices (unrestrained)
Of ancient Medes and Persians.

For bashful couples in despair
Who fear themselves mismated,

The latest marriage manual,
Profusely illustrated.

And here's another picture book
To pique the jaded vision,
The pictures quite legitimate,
Pompeian, not Parisian.

So let us leave the Book Review,
That strangely blended torrent
Of all the news that's fit to print
And all the ads that orrent.

THOUGHTS THOUGHT WHILE RESTING COMFORTABLY IN PHILLIPS HOUSE, MASSACHUSETTS GENERAL HOSPITAL, OVERLOOKING THE CHARLES RIVER

Something, probably diet, seems to have stunted my mental growth,

I can't remember the difference between a valedictorian and a valetudinarian and I suspect that I am both.

In church when confessing my misdeeds, which I am truly distraught to have done,

I begin with those things I have done that I ought not to have done instead of those things I have left undone that I ought to have done.

Sometimes I spell sex s-e-c-k-s, not to be humorous,

Just because I feel it must be plural, it has become so numerous.

Problems of terminology grow more and more knotty;

I had just learned to say judo instead of jujitsu when it suddenly turned into karate.

I can't seem to get in step;

I know that a policeman is now fuzz instead of a cop, but which does that knowledge make me, hip or hep?

I had just straightened out Guinea and Guiana,

And up popped Ghana.

My mind obviously needs renewal;

Come cosset me with posset, comfort me with comfits, refuel me with gruel.

There, that's bettter, now my mind takes a spry turn,
I remember the difference between a *pas de deux* and a
padishah, padishah means great king or emperor and
pas de deux means Now it's my turn.
I would be completely recovered but for a recent disappoint-
ment suffered when I distinctly heard Ed Sullivan an-
nounce the appearance of a group of Spanish dentures;
When they turned out to be Spanish dancers I asked the
nurse to switch to a film about a dedicated nurse beset
by topers and wenchers.

WHO PUT THAT SPOKESMAN IN MY WHEEL?

I sing of a man whose last name cannot be revealed,
And for his wife my sympathy is unconcealed.
Indeed I am surprised that she has not yet succumbed to a
seizure,
But she remains placid even when he ingests her hand
lotion believing it to be milk of magnesia.
He can't distinguish the bathmats from the towels,
And on many a morn he brushes his teeth with shaving
cream and smears toothpaste on his jowels.
Where most wives would create one more scene she creates
one less scene
When after forty years of crossword puzzling he still doesn't
know an esne from an Essene.
In political arguments he is apt to confirm Marx when at-
tempting to refute Marx,
And when touring he is either getting arrested because he
mistakes the route marks for the speed limit notices or
getting lost because he mistakes the speed limit notices
for route marks.
He cannot tell you whether Jakarta is in Sukarno or Sukarno
is in Jakarta,
And he has a vague idea that the Parthenon is situated in
Sparta.
Although I cannot reveal his name you must by now have
hit on his profession as a matter of course;
He is quoted daily in the press as a Highly Placed Authorita-
tive Source.

NOTES FOR A DOCUMENTARY
IN SEARCH OF A SPONSOR

. . . A land partly Disney and partly Krafft-Ebing,
With slithy toves gimbling and mome raths outgrabing.
The junior-high nymphets, the grim Golden Agers,
The motorbike black-leather-jacket rampagers,
The surfers who spring from their boards to the airwaves
On Beatlesome discs to emit *mal de mer* waves,
The adenoid groups with their flaming hot rods,
And the addlepate dupes with their multiple gods,
The pitchmen who peddle from neon-lit rostrums
Their political, medical, spiritual nostrums,
The perennial crop of lush Aimée Semples,
The swamis, the psychics, the shrines and the temples,
The prophets in sandals who prey as they preach,
And the gilded narcissists who haunt Muscle Beach.
Then there's kind of a Klan, but in much higher brackets,
Who meet not in sheets, but pongee dinner jackets.
Kissin'-cousins are they to the genuine Klan,
Whose devotion to God leads to hatred of man.
On each dedicate heart when in conclave they sit
"De mortuis nil nisi bonum" is writ,
In translation which proves to their great satisfaction
That the only good Nisei is one killed in action.
They cherish the noble conquistadors' fame
And pronounce like Castilians each Spanish place name;
For tradition and status there isn't a doubt
That the Spanish are in — and the Mexicans out.
Oh, the anile John Birchers, the smooth pseudo-Britons,
The tosspots, the sexpots, the purring sexkittens,

The plush poinsettia acres of acres
Of toddlers in training to be Carroll Bakers,
The moviedom moguls whose Rolls-wise luxuriance
Computer-wise proves that there's profit in prurience
As each tawdry sex-epic reveals that there's no biz,
No, no biz, by Allah, as low biz as show biz.
They bejewel the mountains from foothill to crown
With palazzos that either burn up or slide down.
On TV they expose their delusion unclad
That we all are, like Hollywood, Hollywood-mad.
With the same inside jokes they persistently plague us,
The same jocular hints about boozing and Vegas,
The same jolly feuds 'twixt the same individuals,
The same shameless plugs for each other's residuals,
So when tournament golf turns up on your screen
Only once in a while are the pros to be seen;
With the keen X-ray eye of a high-class embalmer
You must look through Phil Harris to find Arnold Palmer.
There's the thrice-married lamb and the thrice-divorced tup
Who 'neath sunlight and spotlight grow old, but not up,
And coyly elope when new urges inflate them,
Escaping from Zanuck knows who would frustrate them,
All living it up, but when they are through,
Behold Forest Lawn — they can die it up, too . . .

BOTANIST, AROINT THEE!
OR, HENBANE BY ANY OTHER NAME

I had always known that botanists were finicky,
But not until a recent tour of the dictionary did I realize
    that they were also cynicky.
They are friendly toward strangers, they are not xenophobes,
    they enjoy the theater, they are not dramaphobes,
But it is now clear to me that they are, to coin an unscholarly
    but apt neologism, thalamaphobes.
Yes, they are in favor of pollenizing
Just as much as Kosygin is against imperialistic colonizing,
But they disparage marriage.
Let me anticipate your queries,
Let me simply call your attention to the matrimony vine,
    the common name by which they identify a solanaceous
    plant of the genus *Lycium,* cultivated for its flowers,
    foliage and berries.
So far, so innocent, but hold! What is solanaceous? Upon
    my honor,
Included in the species *Solanaceae* what do we find? We
    find henbane, mandrake and belladonna.
Let alone mandrake and belladonna, you know and I know
    that every botanist knows henbane, it's an herb com-
    mon, not exotic;
It bears sticky, hairy foliage of disagreeable odor and has
    properties poisonous and narcotic.
So here we have a plant sticky, hairy, lethal and mephitic,

[95]

and by what name does the botanist choose this plant
    to define?
The matrimony vine.
I say, Lady, if you wish of all wives to be the forgottenist,
Marry a botanist.

YOU ARE OLD,
FATHER BERTRAND

Bertrand said to
a lyndon his
eye he had pinned
on, "Let's
both go
to law: I
will prose-
cute *you.* —
I do not
stand alone,
but with Sartre
and Simone,
and a vol-
uble French
intellectual crew."
Said the
lyndon, "Dear me,
such a
trial would
be, with
no jury
or judge,
a ju-
dicative
mess."
"We'll be
judge,
We'll be
jury,"
said
Ber-
trand
with fury:
"And our
verdict
has
just
been
released
to the
press."

MR. MINIKIN'S WAKING
NIGHTMARE
OR, WHAT WILL BE WON'T BE

My friend Mr. Minikin is in a swivet.

He has learned how a marriage can suddenly go wrong as
four martinis before lunch just when it seems right as
a trivet.

Any city editor wishing to cover all the phases of his be-
wilderment would need half a dozen legmen,

Because the vagaries of the feminine mind have got under
his skin, shell, rind, integument or tegmen.

He feels as if he were within the perimeter

Of a whirling invisible scimitar.

Mr. and Mrs. Minikin had loaded their car with bikinis,
baby oil, orange doe skin slacks, floppy hats, rhinestone-
studded glasses and other staples,

And they were en route to Key West or Sarasota or possibly
Naples,

And somewhere near Tappahannock on the Rappahannock
or some place equally euphonial,

Why, Mrs. Minikin spotted an antique shop in which she
was sure she could pick up for a song some unique
item baronial or colonial,

But by the time she had mentioned this to Mr. Minikin the
treasure house was half a mile behind,

And when he offered to turn around and go back she just
said, No, no, never mind.

He sensed that she was displeased and he said *Mea Culpa*
and I'm sorry, and also It's all my fault,

And he assured her that turning around would be a pleasure
and she said No, she knew antiques bored him, so
hurry up or he'd miss that supper of chitlins, cornpone,
pot licker, red-eye gravy and celery salt.

He then promised her faithfully that they would halt at
that very antique shop on their way home eight weeks
hence,

And that was when he was clobbered by a verb inflection
unknown to males or grammarians, the future imperfect
tense.

After a jiffy journey in her time machine she accused him
of going to not have stopped at that or any other
antique shop for ever and ever, and thereby achieved
an object as unique as sublime;

By not speaking to him again until they were below Charles-
ton she managed to let the present actual punishment
precede the future potential crime.

TELL ME NO FIBLETS, WHERE ARE THE GIBLETS?

The magazines for ladies are all of one accord:
The hostess is the priestess of the festive board.
They tell us half the story, but they do not tell it all,
No, they won't name the priestess with the leastess on the
    ball.
She's the priestess in the autumn when the leaves are turn-
    ing gold
Who will not serve the syrup till the cakes are cold,
And reveals herself at Christmas as the leastess priestess yet,
For she won't bring out the gravy till the turkey's been et.

The oysters in the silky soup have scalded every tongue,
And now a breathless silence envelops old and young.
The turkey's on the table like a monarch on his throne,
Majestic as a mountain, and arid as a bone,
And every eye is wider as the carving knife is flourished,
And every mouth is open to be succulently nourished.
The vegetables in full array are piled upon your plate,
You take your knife, you take your fork, and then you sit
    and wait.

You gaze upon the white meat, you gaze upon the dark,
Your gaze does not deceive you, they are turning stiff and
    stark.
The creamy mashed potatoes grow rigid and congealed,
But hunger overcomes you, and sulkily you yield.
You tackle sawdust stuffing, you toy with chilly peas,
And then behold your hostess, complacent as you please.

She doesn't say "Excuse me," she doesn't cry "Peccavi,"
But when you've choked on everything, she passes out the
gravy.

Pass the gravy, pretty priestess, for I am waxing wroth,
I have no food to put it on, I'll pour it on the cloth.
If you hadn't wished to see me run amuckish and berserky
You should have put the gravy out before you put the turkey.

WE'RE FINE, JUST FINE
OR, YOU'LL BE ASTONISHED WHEN
I'M GONE, YOU RASCAL, YOU

Some people slowly acquire a healthy glowing complexion
    by sitting for weeks on a beach surrounded by surfers
    and seagulls,
And others acquire it rapidly by downing a couple of hefty
    Chivas Regulls,
But whether a healthy glowing complexion is acquired
    openly or by stealth,
It is not always an indication of health.
Your life expectancy may be minus,
You are a seething mass of symptoms, from astragalus to
    sinus,
But if you have a healthy glowing complexion your friends
    cannot hold their congratulations in abeyance;
They lose no opportunity to inform you that you are in the
    pink, when you are as far from the pink as something
    summoned up at a séance.
Truly, who needs a physician
When every friend is a diagnostician?
And as for the physician himself, who tells you that you
    could go ten rounds with Muhammad Ali, simply be-
    cause your cheeks are ruddy as a pippin,
Why, I'd as soon consult Dr. Pangloss or Dr. Crippen.
I share the resentment of Shakespeare, who obviously wrote
    Sonnet CXL after an evening devoted to sack and
    malmsey,
And the house physician at the Globe congratulated him on
    his healthy exterior glow, when his interior was in-
    sufferably queasy and qualmsy.

Avaunt, healthy exterior glow!
"Testy sick men," wrote the indignant poet, "when their
deaths be near, no news but health from their physi-
cians know."
I can guess why Mr. W.H. was honored as the Sonnets' onlie
begetter;
Mr. W.H. alone of Shakespeare's companions didn't slap
him on the back when he was feeling awful and tell him
he had never looked better.

HOOK, LINE AND ENNUI

The fisherman, oh the fisherman,
That sportsman piscatorial,
Has anesthetized his fellow man
For ages immemorial.
As his ancient prototype was wont
In the days of Hammurabi,
Be the talk of cabbages or kings,
He turns it to his hobby.
When my taxes rise, I blame the lobbyist;
When my eyelids droop I blame the hobbyist.

The bible of the fisherman tribe
Looms like a rock Gibraltan,
The Com-pleat Angler is its name,
Its author, Isaak Walton.
This overlord of fin and gill
Whose dicta they obey yet,
He spelled "complete" compleatly wrong,
And "Isaac" with a K yet.
I heard a little birdie twitter it;
The fisherman's god was semiliterate.

The fisherman's gift of total recall,
His reminiscing chronic,
Make the Ancient Mariner himself
Seem taciturn and laconic.
I do not disbelieve his tales
Of steelhead by the thousand,
I do not tell him to his face
I think I'm being Münchausend,

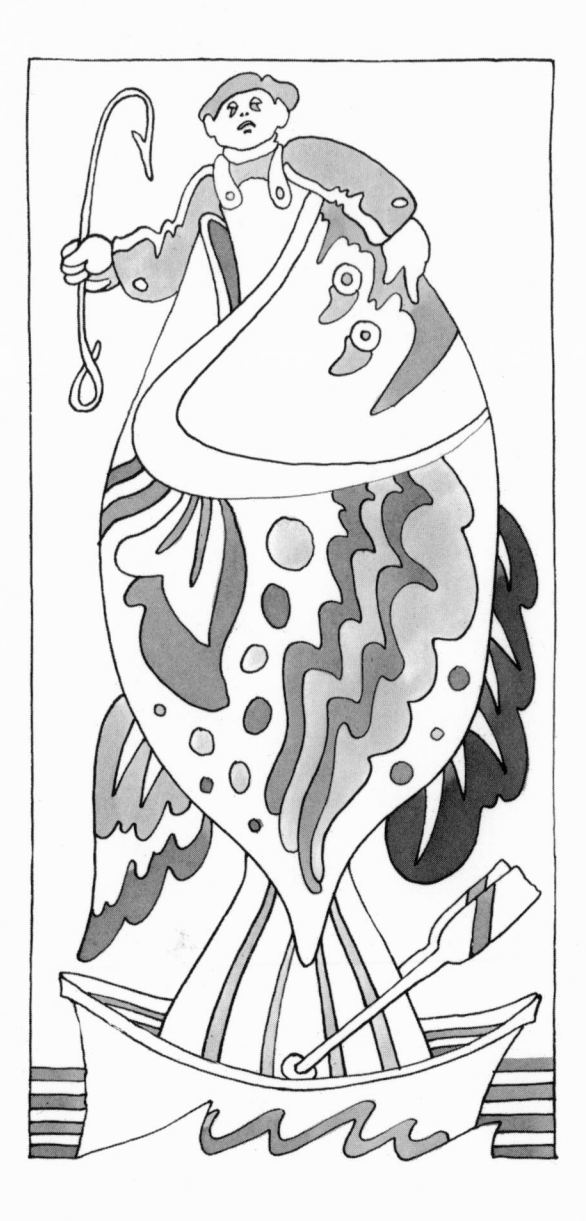

But Charles Perrault and the Brothers Grimm
Were amateurs compared to him.

I concede that the fisherman is behooved
By Fate, the Great Behoover,
To pit his wiles against the trout
And the salmon to outmaneuver,
That he played the sailfish dawn to dusk
That hangs o'er his mantelshelf,
But he won't concede that the epic thrills
Nobody but himself.
Once, cornered, buttonholed and prodded
By a fisherman, that's when Homer nodded.

The fisherman is a worthy man,
Not given to misprision,
But he washes the scales from off his hands
And not from off his vision.
He may have won a master's degree
From M.I.T. or Fordham,
But he can't perceive that one man's fish
Is another fellow's boredom.
Now let me tell you a real dumfounder —
How my clam got stolen by a flounder.

I'M NO SAINT, AND I HAVE MY DOUBTS ABOUT VALENTINE, TOO

Saint Valentine, as is known to everyone who has consulted
an encyclopedia, was martyred in the year 270, prob-
ably 270 A.D.,

Because there weren't any saints, only prophets, in B.C.

His career is shrouded in mists which I have been unable
to dissipate,

But his martyrdom is an ordeal in which I am now annually
compelled to participate.

Valentine's Day presented few problems when the Gish
sisters were young and the movies were silent and
flickerish,

And an infatuated little boy didn't rely on a sports car and
a credit card to further his suit, just a paper bag of
bull's-eyes or horehound drops or shoestrings of licker-
ish.

Falling in love was as simple as a dimple.

At this point I hear the jeers of some ultramodern challenger,

And I freely admit that my adolescence reminds me more
of Tarkington than of Salinger,

But such innocence made life easier for victims of the Valen-
tine habit;

All you had to do was take a sheet of paper and draw a
heart with an arrow through it carrying the words "I
love you," and sign it "Guess who," and shove it under
the front door of your only beloved and run like a
rabbit.

One girl, one Valentine, and that was it.

I should have, while I was ahead of the game, quit.

Yes, I should have quit while I was ahead,

Because today a person is expected to distribute Valentines like campaign literature or free samples of some new exotic calorie-free spread.

The world is so overflowing with love that a person is expected to present his entire clan with some affectionate token,

And you have to clamber up and down your family tree to be sure that every sensitive heart remains unbroken,

Because if any one of them fails to receive a missive attractive, ingenious, and different from everybody else's, why Saint Valentine is who you have violated the law of,

And she looks at you like a spaniel that you have unwittingly stepped on the paw of.

The way the custom is spreading begins to pass belief,

I fear that on some future Valentine's Day I shall be expected to pay tribute to my butcher, my baker, my lawyer, my beggarman and my friendly neighborhood Indian chief.

The more I consider my heritage from Saint Valentine the more I understand why the heathen never stood for him,

And whatever they did, whether they strung him up by the thumbs or rolled him downhill in a barrel, I still think it was entirely too good for him.

BACKWARD, TURN BACKWARD, O COMMENTATOR, IN THY FLIGHTS

There is almost no major-league city in which I have not sat
around a hotel room with time to spare,
And innumerable are the ball games I have listened to on
the air.
Innumerable also are the announcers who of ineptness are
the quintessence,
Although they have the virtue of recalling to me the van-
ished and sometimes golden days of my pre-adoles-
cence.
Their terminology was stale even when the natty fan in
moments of ecstasy stamped on his brown derby hat;
I get the feeling that either Dick Rover or Napoleon Lajoie
will be next at bat.
I hear the rattle of tin Lizzies and flivvers
When I am told that the hurler kicks, rocks, and either deals
or delivers.
I am again a tan-cheeked boy with no socks
When the gardener first backpedals, then commits a miscue,
and allows the runner to dent the platter as Pale Hose
bow to Bosox.
It's a brand-new ball game and I am an openmouthed child
When with two on, two out, and a count of two and two
I learn that it's deuces wild.
I will say for the announcers that in Latin American pro-
nunciation they are completely or even too completely
versed.
It gives me infinite pleasure to know that Hozay is on third,
Hayzoos is on second and — shades of Abbott and
Costello — Hoolio's on first.

A MAN CAN COMPLAIN,
CAN'T HE?
(A LAMENT FOR THOSE WHO THINK OLD)

Pallid and moonlike in the smog,
Now feeble Phoebus 'gins arise;
The upper floors of Empire State
Have vanished into sooty skies.
Half missing, like the shrouded tower,
Lacklustre, like the paten solar,
I draw reluctant waking breath;
Another day, another dolor.

That breath I draw was first exhaled
By diesel and incinerator;
I should have wakened not at all,
Or, were it feasible, even later.
Walls of the world close in on me,
Threats equatorial and polar;
Twixt pit and pendulum I lie;
Another day, another dolor.

Here's news about the current strike,
The latest, greatest test of fission,
A fatal mugging in the park,
An obit of the Geneva mission.
One envelope yields a baffling form
Submitted by the tax comptroller;
A jury summons completes my mail;
Another day, another dolor.

Once eager for, I've come to dread,
The nimble fingers of my barber;

He's training strands across my scalp
Like skimpy vines across an arbor.
The conversation at the club
Is all intestinal or molar;
What dogs the Class of '24?
Another day, another dolor.

Between the dotard and the brat
My disaffection veers and varies;
Sometimes I'm sick of clamoring youth,
Sometimes of my contemporaries.
I'm old too soon, yet young too long;
Could Swift himself have planned it droller?
Timor vitae conturbat me;
Another day, another dolor.

THE STILLY NIGHT:
A SOPORIFIC REFLECTION

There is one source of marital discord so delicate that I
    approach it on tiptoe,
And it reveals itself when the partners whose melancholy
    boast is that they are insomniacs are really somniacs,
    only not overt but crypto-.
He unwinds himself from the bedclothes each morn and
    piteously proclaims that he didn't sleep a wink, and
    she gives him a glance savage and murderous
And replies that it was she who didn't close an eye until
    cockcrow because of his swinish slumber as evidenced
    by his snores continuous and stertorous,
And his indignation is unconcealed,
He says she must have dreamed that one up during her
    night-long sweet repose, which he was fully conscious
    of because for eight solid hours he had listened to her
    breathing not quite so gentle as a zephyr on a flowery
    field.
Such is the genesis of many a myth,
Because her statement is a falsehood that is akin to truth,
    and his a truth that is to falsehood akith.
The fact is that she did awaken twice for brief intervals
    and he was indeed asleep and snoring, and he did
    awaken similarly and she was indeed unconscious and
    breathing miscellaneously,
But they were never both awake simultaneously.
Oh, sleep it is a blessed thing, but not to those wakeful ones
    who watch their mates luxuriating in it when they feel
    that their own is sorely in arrears.

I am certain that the first words of the Sleeping Beauty to her prince were, "You *would* have to kiss me just when I had dropped off after tossing and turning for a hundred years."

IT'S ALWAYS JUNE IN JANUARY, ALSO VICE VERSA

Shelley once asked whether if winter comes spring can be far behind,

Which was a good question for a poet but would not be asked by any lawyer in his right mind.

Why?

Because it is at once leading and rhetorical, obviously calling for a negative reply.

Today this question would not be posed even by a poet, and for the best of reasons;

In the general speed-up since Shelley's time there has been a telescoping of the seasons.

The once slow-footed calendar is now a sprinter;

Spring and fall have been eliminated, leaving only summer and winter.

Our forefathers marked the end of winter by changing from the forbidding red flannel underclothes they were sewed inside of to lighter and more suggestive ones;

We, by extracting ourselves from festive hibernating resorts and inserting ourselves into festive estive ones.

The winter beach people head mountainward and the winter mountain people head shoreward,

And the patient tradesmen sigh as they mail their bills to customers whose permanent address seems to be "Please forward."

At Bar Harbor ladies celebrate their return from Boca Raton and Coral Gables

By substituting their summer mink for their winter sables.

From Oyster Bay to the Hamptons the loyal local police
force protects the gentry from the touring proletarian
simians;
On Fire Island the beaches are adorned with a colorful
throng of Bohemian Endymions.
At Provincetown the fishermen are frustrated by the swarm
of artists on the docks;
They can't unload their smacks for the smocks,
Indeed the entire population, from Mackinac Island to
Biloxi, from Mount Washington to Mount Rainier,
Is made up of people from one place summering in another
place and deciding to go to a different place next year.

THEY DON'T READ DE QUINCEY
IN PHILLY OR CINCY

Consider, friends, George Joseph Smith,
A Briton not to trifle with,
When wives aroused his greed or wrath
He led them firmly to the bath.
Instead of guzzling in the pub,
He drowned his troubles in the tub.

In France, however, thrifty land,
The bathtub must be filled by hand,
And that is why that fabled fiend,
The laziest ever guillotined,
When shedding his prospective brides
In multiple uxoricides
Just combed his beard and shined his hat
And led them to the Landrumat.

Oh why then doth our home-grown spouse
When tired of mate around the house
Just seize on any weapon handy?
A dreary *modus operandi,*
Proof we belittle in our hearts
Fine murder with the other arts.
As connoisseurs have often snorted,
Murders, like wines, are best imported.

MR. TWOMBLEY'S ULTIMATE TRIUMPH

Once there was a man named Mr. Twombley, and he was
    monarch of all he surveyed;

He had a lovely wife and two lovely children and a lovely
    portfolio of blue-chip stocks and even a lovely cook
    and a lovely maid.

He also had a swimming pool and a barbecue grill and a
    library containing forty-seven titles;

Nevertheless there was a vulture gnawing at his vitals.

Mr. Twombley felt that he had failed to live up to today's
    code of lower, middle, and upper-class living, which
    is as rigid as those of Moses and Hammurabi;

In a word, Mr. Twombley had no hobby.

Yes, the aptitude and even the desire for hobbies had been
    omitted from his being;

Not for him the fascination of golf or tennis, of sailing or
    climbing, of bridge or canasta, or archery or skiing.

Poor hobbyless Mr. Twombley, what words can his loneli-
    ness describe?

He was a second-class citizen, ostentatiously excluded from
    the boastful reminiscent bar and locker-room powwows
    of the tribe;

Because of all snobs, the snobbiest

Is the hobbyist.

But wait! Along came grandfatherhood, and Presto!

Mr. Twombley was transformed into a hobbyist of over-
    powering gusto, not to say zesto.

His wallet bulged with overexposed or underexposed snap-
    shots of human tadpoles middle-sized and small,

And when it came to recounting the details of a hand of old
    maid or slapjack he developed total recall.
He was a treasure-house of infantile cute sayings and an
    authority on the riddle,
And he would have also been an authority on croquet if
    any contest had survived those accusations of cheating
    that break out in the middle.
Yes indeed, Mr. Twombley found a hobby in his grand-
    children, but he was not as completely obsessed by it
    as you might think;
Every time a new grandchild needed a diaper changed he
    disappeared like a chipmunk into a chink.

THE SOLITARY HUNTSMAN

The solitary huntsman
No coat of pink doth wear,
But midnight black from cap to spur
Upon his midnight mare.
He drones a tuneless jingle
In lieu of tally-ho,
"I'll catch a fox
And put him in a box
And never let him go."

The solitary huntsman,
He follows silent hounds,
No horn proclaims his joyless sport,
And never a hoofbeat sounds.
His hundred hounds, his thousands,
Their master's will they know;
To catch a fox
And put him in a box
And never let him go.

For all the fox's doubling
They track him to his den.
The chase may fill a morning,
Or threescore years and ten.
The huntsman never sated
Screaks to his saddlebow,
"I'll catch another fox
And put him in a box
And never let him go."

THE MAN WHO FRUSTRATED
MADISON AVENUE

There was a man named Mr. Patricola,

And one memorable day he turned off his Zenith, or maybe
it was an Admiral or a Motorola.

His boiling point was higher than average

Because, being named Patricola, he had learned to control
his temper when new acquaintances inquired if he was
a sparkling beverage.

He was even as mild as tapioca

When they suggested that he blend with Miss Imogene
Coca,

But something suddenly snapped when the Huntley-
Brinkley report on the seizure of the Moscow radio by
the Chinese was interrupted by an important message
from the sponsor about irregularity delivered by a trio
of off-key sopranos, and his blood began to bubble and
his adrenals tingled;

Mr. Patricola was over-jingled.

He felt like a puny hoplite confronted by a giant Persian,

And he realized that his only chance lay in a campaign of
subversion.

He began by telling his friends that they should chew
Beechnut gum to double their pleasure, double their
fun,

And that Raleighs taste good like a cigarette should, and
Rheingold is the one beer to have when you're having
more than one.

He chanted to a departing friend, "Let Avis put YOU in the
driver's seat today,"

And he advised his various hostesses to serve Chock Full
o'Nuts, the coffier coffee, for finer than which even a
millionaire's money could not pay.
The ripples from these pebbles swept over every Food Fair
and Bohack's and A & P,
And wholesale and retail chaos reigned from Bangor to
what the jingle tune implies is the Blue-tail Fly Wine
Countree.
This situation Mr. Patricola was by the producers taken to
task for
Because the befuddled consumers didn't know what be-
jingled brand to ask for.
His satisfaction was immense,
And he next, as a non-flyer, refused to pay his income tax as
long as any part of his dollar was used by government-
subsidized airlines to serve free meals from Voisin and
"21" at his expense.
He vowed that the Internal Revenue Department would not
see a nickel of his dough
Unless he and his fellow groundlings could enjoy the similar
privilege of free meals from the Colony and Le Pavillon
on the Pennsylvania and the B. & O.
Mr. Patricola now shuts his ears to airborne commercials
and uses only those products advertised in yellowing
magazines bequeathed to him by his ingenuous sires;
He is happily driving a Packard ("Ask the man who owns
one") equipped with Fisk ("Time to re-tire") tires.
He scours it daily with Bon Ami ("Hasn't scratched yet")
and Pears Soap ("Have you a little fairy in your
home?") and his brand of underwear may easily be
guessed —
"Next to myself I like BVD best."
That old French adage is not only pithy but true —
Chacun à son goo.

NEVER WAS I BORN
TO SET THEM RIGHT

Since the non-book and the anti-hero are now accepted
     elements of modern negative living
I feel justified in mentioning a few examples of the march
     of progress for which I suggest a heartfelt non-thanks-
     giving.
I not only like Turkish towels or a reasonable facsimile on
     emerging from the tub,
I also like towels after washing my hands, even paper ones
     that you rip untimely from a reluctant device that
     warns you, Blot, do not rub.
I do not like the contraptions that have replaced towels in
     every washroom from the humblest Howard Johnson
     to the haughtiest Statler or Hilton,
Those abominations which you stand cringingly in front of
     waiting for them to scorch you with a blast of air from
     a hell hotter than any imagined by Dante or Milton.
I like the common incandescent lamp whose light is pro-
     duced in a filament rendered luminous by the passage
     of current through it,
I do not like the fluorescent lamp in which light is produced
     by passage of electricity through a metallic vapor or
     gas enclosed in a tube or bulb, I resent it, I rue it, I
     eschew it.
You stumble into a dark room and press a switch and then
     stand in continuing darkness for half a minute wonder-
     ing if you have blown a fuse sky-high,
And then the fluorescent fixture flickers and hesitates and
     finally lights up and you see your face in the mirror
     and it is yellow and green and purple like a recently
     blackened eye.

I do not like bottle openers shaped like a mermaid or a fish
or even an axolotl,
They may be all right for driving thumbtacks with but
they're no good for opening a bottle.
I do not like the substitution at toll-booths of the electronic
coin-basket for the human collector,
I accept it as grudgingly as Hecuba might have accepted
the substitution of Polyphemus for Hector.
The collector would even lean into your car to accept the
coin from your right hand, but you have to toss it at
the basket with your left,
And I happen to be the least ambidextrous northpaw who
ever chunked a pebble at a newt or an eft.
I do not like the thrifty European airmail stationery com-
bining envelope with letter, I have never faced one but
I trembled;
You need a well-honed paper knife to open it, and even
then end up with eight or sixteen fragments which must
be painstakingly reassembled.
Speaking of envelopes, I particularly dislike in our non-
civilization the return envelope with postage prepaid
which the Internal Revenue Department does not en-
close with its annual demands; of needlessly irritating
the taxpayer this is the most picayune of their many
ways;
When I drain my bank account to write them a check I
think they might at least blow me to a nickel's worth
of postage, especially as it wouldn't cost them anything
anyways.

MODEST MEDITATIONS ON THE HERE, THE HERETOFORE AND THE HEREAFTER

I

Drink deep, old friend, and deeply drown your sorrows,
Perhaps you'll be the first of humankind
For whom they'll not through many turbid morrows
Rise bloated to the surface of the mind.

II

Before the woods were cleared to make the fairways,
Before the sand was hauled to make the bunkers,
Or mole was gassed to smoothe the putting surface,
The red man squatted here upon his hunkers
While precious arrowheads he edged and pointed;
His thoughts were of survival, not of sports,
But could he today resist those tempting targets,
Pumpkin-rumped women in their daughters' shorts?

III

Cry welladay, this world is workaday,
Where are the miracles for which we pray?
Well, miracles, so few and far between,
Must be believed, my brethren, to be seen.

IV

I didn't go to church today,
I trust the Lord to understand.
The surf was swirling blue and white,
The children swirling on the sand.
He knows, He knows how brief my stay,
How brief this spell of summer weather,
He knows when I am said and done
We'll have a plenty of time together.

STICKS AND STONES MAY
BREAK THEIR BONES, BUT
NAMES WILL LOSE A SPONSOR

April is reputedly a heartless month, but for managers of
ball teams September can be sufficiently cruel.

There came a year when Labor Day found the Yankees and
the A's engaged in a mastodonic duel.

They alternated vantage points,

And from day to day first place kept changing hands by a
matter of percentage points.

After the holiday doubleheader,

The Yankees couldn't have looked deader.

Three players drawing over $75,000 annually came up with
pulled hamstrings — the occupational hazard in the
$75,000 bracket —

And a $60,000 pitcher got bursitis after he was so excited at
being intentionally passed that he forgot to put on his
jacket.

A $45,000 infielder was hospitalized with sinus,

And a host of unpredictable disasters overtook those regu-
lars who were drawing down $35,000 or maybe a grand
or two plus or minus.

Consider a typical case:

The diamond was so littered with papers that a $37,500
runner broke his ankle sliding into Art Buchwald's
column, which he mistook for second base.

Well, the chief of the farm system assured the Yankee man-
ager that he needn't yet look forward to wearing resoled
shoes and multicolored knee patches;

He said they had a bunch of athletes on the Richmond Club
who were churnin' up the chitlins and tearin' up the
pea patches.

He said everything would be just fine —

The team batting average was .341, and the fielding average
was .996, and the earned-run average was 0.9.

The manager said to bring them up, for this heartening
news corresponded with his aims,

And he asked what were some of these wonders' names.

Well, their names were Joe Schlitz and Chuck Pabst and
Jim Chesterfield and Phil Morris and Dino Sinclair and
Scooter Texaco

And Willie Kent and Sam Schaefer and a real comer named
José Löwenbräu, from Mexico.

What was the manager's answer?

Okay with me if it's okay with the sponsor.

That's how the Yankees out the pennant race did tumble;

They finished the season with three inept but aptly named
outfielders — Campbell Reynolds, Smiley Ballantine,
and Happy Humble.

WHO SAYS IT'S SO NICE TO HAVE A MAN AROUND THE HOUSE?

Here's a biography condensed
Of one the cards are stacked against,
Who daily endures afflictions rougher
Than early martyr had to suffer.
He prefaces each just complaint
By admitting that he's not a saint,
(A point unargued by his friends)
And then his list of "buts" appends,
Superlatives pejorative
Pronounced in tone authoritive.

His dentist is the brutalest,
His doctor is the futilest,
His symptoms are the lethalest,
His aches the funeral wreathalest,
His viruses the snidest,
The unidentifiedest,
His holidays the rainiest,
With chiggers subcutaniest,
It's he Fate hounds the fervidest,
Hangovers undeservidest,

His telephone gone Dada-ist,
Its busy buzz cicada-est,
His morning mail mishmashiest,
The postage-duest trashiest,
He draws the waiter snootiest
And hails the cabs off-dutiest,

His tax unfairest, stupidest,
Cupidity at its cupidest,
In short, he's ready to write a tome
Entitled "Universe Go Home."

O Justice, of all from whom thou fleddest
He is the should-have-stood-in-beddest.
Who is this happy worrier? Who?
One every wife is married to.

PERMISSIVE PICTURES PRESENTS "HAPPY HALLOWEEN, EVERYBODY," AN ALFRED HITCHCOCK PRODUCTION

There is an old hymn that now arouses my curiosity as well
    as my zest,
Which is the one that begins, For all thy saints who from
    their labors rest.
May the memory of all the saints be forever green,
But I wonder how much rest they actually get on the Eve
    of All Saints Day, known as Halloween.
I can remember when children got an adequate thrill from
    ringing doorbells, or rigging ticktacks on the window,
    or even bobbing for apples,
While they now amuse themselves by upsetting gravestones
    and desecrating chapels.
I try to refrain from crabbedness and contentiousness and
    general fly-off-the-handleism,
But I find it difficult when the young have ceased to dis-
    tinguish between mischief and vandalism.
What has become of the old-fashioned urchin who terrified
    his cooperative relatives with the aid of an old sheet
    and a lighted pumpkin?
He has given way to a savage and malicious breed com-
    pounded of country slicker and city bumpkin.
On Halloween it's not the ghoulies and ghosties and long-
    legged beasties that put my peace of mind to flight,
It's the things that go bump in the night.
I am by now something of a cynic;

I suspect that any bumps in the night of Halloween are less
likely to be caused by hobgoblins or bogles than by
juveniles rolling a full garbage pail over a fence and
into a swimming pool, or tossing a cherry bomb into
the ambulance carrying an emergency patient to the
clinic.
These are my glummer thoughts, but I have others that are
not so glum,
One of which is that too often the only visible part of the
pond of youth is the scum.
My hope continues undimmed
That inevitably the scum will be skimmed.
With such thoughts in mind I firmly expect that on some
future All Saints Eve all the saints will enjoy undis-
turbed rest from their labors,
And so, I selfishly add, will I and my neighbors.

THE QUACK FROWN SOX
LUMPS OVEN THE · ·,
OR, FAREWELL, PHI BETA KAFKA

If my mind is wandery,

Well, I'm in a quandary.

I am recovering from a temporary secretary, a girl from Bennington,

Who neither resembled nor had heard of such dream girls of my youth as Louise Groody or Ann Pennington.

She came to me under the misapprehension that she could thereby pick up experience in an easy school, not a hard school,

Which would lead her to producing and directing off-Broadway plays of the avant-, or prenez-garde school.

Her eyes and her conversation glistened,

But she never listened.

When she encountered such a Nordic name as Georg she carefully pronounced it Gay-org,

But when transcribing a reference to *The Raven* she typed it *Mr. Raven,* which led me into fruitless speculation as to what Thornton Burgess would have named the ape in *Murders in the Rue Morgue.*

I played Polonius to this pixie, plying her with admonitions both as a kindly pa and as a harsh pa,

But when I handed her a package for Parcel Post she sent it Marcel Proust, as I only realized when it eventually returned to me stamped *Marcel Proust ne marche pas.*

To sum up, let me say that I am at present capable of living, or viable,

But I am also easily crumbled or reduced to powder, which is friable.

Being both viable and friable I wish to prolong my existence,
　　not to wreck it,
And I am now looking for a good listener who just squeaked
　　through high school in Feeble Bluff, Nebraska, and
　　never heard of Joyce or Samuel Beckett.

THE JOYOUS MALINGERER

Who is the happy husband? Why, indeed
'Tis he who's useless in the time of need;
Who, asked to unclasp a bracelet or a necklace,
Contrives to be utterly futile, fumbling, feckless,
Or when a zipper nips his loved one's back
Cannot restore the zipper to its track.
Another time, not wishing to be flayed,
She will not use him as a lady's maid.

Stove-wise he's the perpetual backward learner
Who can't turn on or off the proper burner.
If faced with washing up he never gripes,
But simply drops more dishes than he wipes.
She finds his absence preferable to his aid,
And thus all meal time chores doth he evade.

He can, attempting to replace a fuse,
Black out the coast from Boston to Newport News,
Or, hanging pictures, be the rookie wizard
Who fills the parlor with a plaster blizzard.
He'll not again be called to competition
With decorator or with electrician.

At last it dawns upon his patient spouse
He's better at his desk than round the house.

VERY NICE, REMBRANDT, BUT HOW ABOUT A LITTLE MORE COLOR?

The world is too full of people whom were I their parent
    I would ruthlessly disown.
They are those who cannot leave well alone.
Indeed, there is no limit to the impudence of these tasteless
    noddies;
Far from leaving well alone, when confronted with the best
    they become the most meddlesome of Matties, the
    busiest of bodies.
It is scarcely two centuries since there flourished a cult of
    pedantic prigs and prudes who should have had their
    quill pens washed with soap;
It was their aim to transmute pure Shakespeare into adulter-
    ated Pope.
I thought that here the compulsion to improve the unim-
    provable had reached its acme,
Sort of like the Bell Song from Lakmé,
But no, we now have another movement for improvement
    bent on fluoridating the springs Pierian.
It is equally irksome, even though its grotesqueries do not
    run to the Shakespearean.
This is the personality cult developed by our popular re-
    cording artists, both vocalists and wielders of batons,
And they have perfected a method of making geese from
    swans.
It consists, both here and in Britain,
Of simply not performing the song as written.
The arranger takes a superior look at the original Gershwin
    melodic or tempo line

And rearranges the arrangement while bouncing on a
     trampoline.
And how can you be even satiric
About the singer who sets out to point up a Porter lyric?
There is a current version of "Just One of Those Things"
     as emended by a songstress of renown
In which she corrects the phrasing and ruins the rhythm
     by shouting, "We'd have been aware that our love
     affair was too *darned* hot not to cool down."
This particular example truly puts the whole process of
     lily-painting on the spot;
If Mr. Porter had wanted to write "too darned hot" instead
     of "too hot" he would have written "too darned hot," as
     we may deduce from the fact that he later did so in a
     song called "Too Darned Hot."
Let us then improve the wording of Bulwer-Lytton by re-
     marking that in the lexicon of lily-painters there is no
     such word as shame.
O Liberty, how many liberties are taken in thy name!

THE STRANGE CASE OF
MRS. MOODUS'S SECOND
HONEYMOON
OR, HOW TO UNOBSTREPERIZE A HUSBAND

Once there was a man named Mr. Rory Moodus, and I do
not envy his wife her plight,

Because as a chivalrous husband he proved to be a verray
unparfit ungentil knight.

He was always quoting Noel Coward to the effect that a
woman should be struck regularly, like a gong,

And at social gatherings he would loudly announce that he
was a fair-minded man who would never argue with
his wife, except that she was always wrong.

He also proclaimed that insurance rates would be in-
tolerably swollen

If patient husbands didn't eventually turn up ninety-five
per cent of the objects their wives claimed were lost or
stolen.

His wit was elementry;

He referred to eligible bachelors as unlanded gentry.

His concept of natural laws could not have been eerier;

When he and his wife shared the same cantaloupe or grape-
fruit he would complain that his half was inferior.

Once when she said someone had told her she looked like
So-and-so, did he say, "Oh, you're prettier than her,"
as any normal husband would do?

Not Mr. Moodus; he said, "Nonsense, she's much homelier
than you."

At this point Mrs. Moodus struck him a glancing blow with
a bust of the ancient British chief Caractacus;

The only reason she failed to bean him, she was a long-suffering woman and was consequently rather out of practacus.

Mr. Moodus was impressed by her spunkiness if not by her marksmanship and realized that this was the woman he loved;

She was demon enough to be iron-clawed and angel enough to be velvet-gloved.

He began to court her anew, and on her throat and wrists he would clasp gems, and at her feet he would scatter gems,

And Mrs. Moodus kept him toeing the mark forever after through judicious use of feminine tactics, reinforced by occasional timely Lysistratagems.

THE SUNSET YEARS OF
SAMUEL SHY

Master I may be,
But not of my fate.
Now come the kisses, too many too late.
Tell me, O Parcae,
For fain would I know,
Where were these kisses three decades ago?
Girls there were plenty,
Mint julep girls, beer girls,
Gay younger married and headstrong career girls,
The girls of my friends
And the wives of my friends,
Some smugly settled and some at loose ends,
Sad girls, serene girls,
Girls breathless and turbulent,
Debs cosmopolitan, matrons suburbulent,
All of them amiable,
All of them cordial,
Innocent rousers of instincts primordial,
But even though health and wealth
Hadn't yet missed me,
None of them,
Not even Jenny,
Once kissed me.

These very same girls
Who with me have grown older
Now freely relax with a head on my shoulder,
And now come the kisses,
A flood in full spate,

The meaningless kisses, too many too late.
They kiss me hello,
They kiss me goodbye,
Should I offer a light, there's a kiss for reply.
They kiss me at weddings,
They kiss me at wakes,
The drop of a hat is less than it takes.
They kiss me at cocktails,
They kiss me at bridge,
It's all automatic, like slapping a midge.
The sound of their kisses
Is loud in my ears
Like the locusts that swarm every seventeen years.

I'm arthritic, dyspeptic,
Potentially ulcery,
And weary of kisses by custom compulsory.
Should my dear ones commit me
As senile demential,
It's from kisses perfunctory, inconsequential.
Answer, O Parcae,
For fain would I know,
Where were these kisses three decades ago?